Presented to:

....

From:

....

JESSE & KARA
BIRKEY

Daily Devotional

4 Keys to Hearing God

"My sheep hear My voice," said Jesus of Nazareth. As you read the journaling in this book, you will agree that Jesse and Kara Birkey surely do hear the voice of their Master. The neat thing is, this book is going to draw you into hearing God's voice daily also!

Each journal entry is followed by a Scripture verse and then the opportunity for you to hear God's voice yourself and journal out what God is speaking to you. What a gift!

This book draws you into dialogue with Almighty God, where you hear His voice, see His visions, receive His counsel, and experience His healing. What could be better?

I encourage you to apply the folowing four keys to hearing God's voice. They work! You will be able to hear His voice if you will use all four together at one time. If they feel a bit awkward at first, don't let that hinder you. Every new skill feels awkward the first several times you do it. You know that practice will makes anything easier. Press on into hearing God's voice because hearing just beats not hearing.

The night I began using these four keys and hearing God's voice, I had a dream showing how awkward I felt. In the dream, I had a new job (i.e. my new job of using the four keys to hearing Gods voice). I was the caretaker of a house, and I was riding a horse up and down the stairs as I was doing my job. Wow! A horse on the stairway. That is like a bull in the china cabinet. That is exactly what I felt like.

I did feel awkward using those four keys. I was practicing picturing Jesus present with me (Acts 2:25) and then tuning to flow (Jn. 7:37-39) and writing. The dream was encouraging because it told me that if I stuck

Come ALIVE with Jesus

JESSE & KARA
BIRKEY

Daily Devotional

From the Authors

Kara and I never planned on writing a devotional. For years we'd been jotting down small portions from our interaction with the Lord and posting them on social media to encourage others. It never occurred to us to take it a step further and compile what we were hearing from God into a book.

That is until one day I (Jesse) received a random comment on Facebook from someone who wondered if I was ever going to organize my posts into a devotional. Kara then shared with me that God had laid the very same thing on her heart the day before. I've discovered that sometimes we need a little outside help to understand what God would like us to do. That random comment from Facebook tipped us off.

Our hearts lit up at the idea of a daily devotional. We felt the Holy Spirit stir inside of us and knew that the words we were hearing from God everyday needed to be available to encourage and spark LIFE into as many people as we could reach.

A critical piece of our foundation with God is our ability to hear him. Hearing the voice of God should be Christianity 101. Unfortunately, most of us have a long history of church attendance without ever feeling like we were present for that class. It's like Ben Stein taking roll call in Ferris Bueller's Day Off – Bueller…Bueller…nope, absent.

Many of us have felt that there have only been a few times in our entire lives in which we heard God speak. Kara and I want to introduce you to his voice. For some it will be for the first time, and for others it might reveal a different tone or aspect of his heart. But for all it will be encouraging, uplifting, and LIFE-giving. Hope will be restored, peace found, and fear conquered. Every day you will encounter a word from the Lord that is for you personally and you will be renewed and refreshed.

We are confident that God's ultimate desire is to grow a deep, intimate relationship with each one of us. There is no benefit to experiencing the *wow* with God without considering how to grow with him beyond where we are now.

That's why we are so excited to have Richard Mull and Dr. Mark Virkler contribute practical steps that will teach you how to continue the dialogue with God past the final sentence each day. These are two mighty men of God who have devoted their lives to showing us how to reach the inner most portions of God's heart. The wisdom they have shared is valuable beyond measure. Grab it and don't let go.

The most important part of this devotional is not the daily word from the Lord, but the intimate communication and relationship that it will spark. It is our desire that the daily word from God be a spring board to propel a new level of intimacy with Him. Set your heart free with God and rejoice in the abundant LIFE he pours in.

Blessings,
Jesse and Kara Birkey

*Throughout this devotional "LIFE" in all caps indicates abundance, worth, value, significance, and love.

ᴼᶜ 4 Keys to Hearing God ᴼᴰ

"My sheep hear My voice," said Jesus of Nazareth. As you read the journaling in this book, you will agree that Jesse and Kara Birkey surely do hear the voice of their Master. The neat thing is, this book is going to draw you into hearing God's voice daily also!

Each journal entry is followed by a Scripture verse and then the opportunity for you to hear God's voice yourself and journal out what God is speaking to you. What a gift!

This book draws you into dialogue with Almighty God, where you hear His voice, see His visions, receive His counsel, and experience His healing. What could be better?

I encourage you to apply the folowing four keys to hearing God's voice. They work! You will be able to hear His voice if you will use all four together at one time. If they feel a bit awkward at first, don't let that hinder you. Every new skill feels awkward the first several times you do it. You know that practice will makes anything easier. Press on into hearing God's voice because hearing just beats not hearing.

The night I began using these four keys and hearing God's voice, I had a dream showing how awkward I felt. In the dream, I had a new job (i.e. my new job of using the four keys to hearing Gods voice). I was the caretaker of a house, and I was riding a horse up and down the stairs as I was doing my job. Wow! A horse on the stairway. That is like a bull in the china cabinet. That is exactly what I felt like.

I did feel awkward using those four keys. I was practicing picturing Jesus present with me (Acts 2:25) and then tuning to flow (Jn. 7:37-39) and writing. The dream was encouraging because it told me that if I stuck with this new job it would take me up a flight of stairs. Hearing God's voice will take one to a higher place in Him. I sure believed that was true. So I didn't quit. I continued on, and it did become easier each day.

Yes, you could get through life spiritually deaf, but you don't need to. Jesus's guarantee is "*My sheep hear My voice.*" His voice is as simple as quieting yourself down, picturing Jesus at your right hand, asking Him to share His heart with you, recognizing His voice as flowing, spontaneous thoughts, and writing them down. As you write in faith, the flow continues. You wait to test it till the flow is done. Never test during the writing process. During the flow, you maintain your stance of faith, for it is faith which allows you to receive from God.

God revealed these four keys to me 25 years ago. Hearing from Him for 25 years has improved my marriage, my health, my finances, my ministry, and my love for Him. It will for you also.

You can expect to receive daily comfort, encouragement, and faith as you journal. I pray God's richest blessing on you as you hear His voice. It will transform your life!

HOW TO HEAR GOD'S VOICE

She had done it again! Instead of coming straight home from school like she was supposed to, she had gone to her friend's house. Without permission. Without our knowledge. Without doing her chores.

With a ministering household that included remnants of three struggling families plus our own toddler and newborn, my wife simply couldn't handle all the work on her own. Everyone had to pull their own weight. Everyone had age-appropriate tasks they were expected to complete. At fourteen, Rachel and her younger brother were living with us while her parents tried to overcome lifestyle patterns that had resulted in the children running away to escape the dysfunction. I felt sorry for Rachel, but, honestly my wife was my greatest concern.

Now Rachel had ditched her chores to spend time with her friends. It wasn't the first time, but if I had anything to say about it, it would be the last. I intended to lay down the law when she got home and make it very clear that if she was going to live under my roof, she would obey my rules.

But…she wasn't home yet. And I had recently been learning to hear God's voice more clearly. Maybe I should try to see if I could hear anything from Him about the situation. Maybe He could give me a way to get her to do what she was supposed to (i.e. what I wanted her to do). So I went to my office and reviewed what the Lord had been teaching me from Habakkuk 2:1,2: "I will stand on my guard post and station myself on the rampart; And I will keep watch to see what He will speak to me…Then the Lord answered me and said, 'Record the vision….'"

Habakkuk said, "I will stand on my guard post…" (Hab. 2:1). **The first key to hearing God's voice is to go to a quiet place and still our own thoughts and emotions.** Psalm 46:10 encourages us to be still, let go, cease striving, and know that He is God. In Psalm 37:7 we are called to "be still before the Lord and wait patiently for Him." There is a deep inner knowing in our spirits that each of us can experience when we quiet our flesh and our minds. Practicing the art of biblical meditation helps silence the outer noise and distractions clamoring for our attention.

I didn't have a guard post but I did have an office, so I went there to quiet my temper and my mind. Loving God through a quiet worship song is one very effective way to become still. In 2 Kings 3, Elisha needed a word from the Lord so he said, "Bring me a minstrel," and as the minstrel played, the Lord spoke. I have found that playing a worship song on my autoharp is the quickest way for me to come to stillness. I need to choose my song carefully; boisterous songs of praise do not bring me to stillness, but rather gentle songs that express my love and worship. And it isn't enough just to sing the song into the cosmos – I come into the Lord's presence most quickly and easily when I use my godly imagination to see the truth that He is right here with me and I sing my songs to Him, personally.

"I will keep watch to see," said the prophet. To receive the pure word of God, it is very important that my heart be properly focused as I become still, because my focus is the source of the intuitive flow. If I fix my eyes upon Jesus (Heb. 12:2), the intuitive flow comes from Jesus. But if I fix my gaze upon some desire of my heart, the intuitive flow comes out of that desire. To have a pure flow I must become still and carefully fix my eyes upon Jesus. Quietly worshiping the King and receiving out of the stillness that follows quite easily accomplishes this.

So I used **the second key to hearing God's voice: As you pray, fix the eyes of your heart upon Jesus, seeing in the Spirit the dreams and visions of Almighty God.** Habakkuk was actually looking for vision as he prayed. He opened the eyes of his heart, and looked into the spirit world to see what God wanted to show him.

God has always spoken through dreams and visions, and He specifically said that they would come to those upon whom the Holy Spirit is poured out (Acts 2:1-4, 17).

Being a logical, rational person, observable facts that could be verified by my physical senses were the foundations of my life, including my spiritual life. I had never thought of opening the eyes of my heart and looking for vision. However, I have come to believe that this is exactly what God wants me to do. He gave me eyes in my heart to see in the spirit the vision and movement of Almighty God. There is an active spirit world all around us, full of angels, demons, the Holy Spirit, the omnipresent Father, and His omnipresent Son, Jesus. The only reasons for me not to see this reality are unbelief or lack of knowledge.

In his sermon in Acts 2:25, Peter refers to King David's statement: "I saw the Lord always in my presence; for He is at my right hand, so that I will not be shaken." The original psalm makes it clear that this was a decision of David's, not a constant supernatural visitation: "I have set (literally, I have placed) the Lord continually before me; because He is at my right hand, I will not be shaken" (Ps.16:8). Because David knew that the Lord was always with him, he determined in his spirit to *see* that truth with the eyes of his heart as he went through life, knowing that this would keep his faith strong.

In order to see, we must look. Daniel saw a vision in his mind and said, "I was looking...I kept looking...I kept looking" (Dan. 7:2, 9, 13). As I pray, I look for Jesus, and I watch as He speaks to me, doing and saying the things that are on His heart. Many Christians will find that if they will only look, they will see. Jesus is Emmanuel, God with us (Matt. 1:23). It is as simple as that. You can see Christ present with you because Christ is present with you. In fact, the vision may come so easily that you will be tempted to reject it, thinking that it is just you. But if you persist in recording these visions, your doubt will soon be overcome by faith as you recognize that the content of them could only be birthed in Almighty God.

Jesus demonstrated the ability of living out of constant contact with God, declaring that He did nothing on His own initiative, but only what He saw the Father doing, and heard the Father saying (Jn. 5:19,20,30). What an incredible way to live!

Is it possible for us to live out of divine initiative as Jesus did? Yes! We must simply fix our eyes upon Jesus. The veil has been torn, giving access into the immediate presence of God, and He calls us to draw near (Lk. 23:45; Heb. 10:19-22). "I pray that the eyes of your heart will be enlightened...."

When I had quieted my heart enough that I was able to picture Jesus without the distractions of my own ideas and plans, I was able to "keep watch to see what He will speak to me." I wrote down my question: "Lord, what should I do about Rachel?"

Immediately the thought came to me, "She is insecure." Well, that certainly wasn't my thought! Her behavior looked like rebellion to me, not insecurity.

But like Habakkuk, I was coming to know the sound of God speaking to me (Hab. 2:2). Elijah described it as a still, small voice (I Kings 19:12). I had previously listened for an inner audible voice, and God does speak that way at times. However, I have found that usually, God's voice comes as spontaneous thoughts, visions, feelings, or impressions.

For example, haven't you been driving down the road and had a thought come to you to pray for a certain person? Didn't you believe it was God telling you to pray? What did God's voice sound like? Was it an audible voice, or was it a spontaneous thought that lit upon your mind?

Experience indicates that we perceive spirit-level communication as spontaneous thoughts, impressions and visions, and Scripture confirms this in many ways. For example, one definition of *paga*, a Hebrew word for intercession, is "a chance encounter or an accidental intersecting." When God lays people on our hearts, He does it through paga, a chance-encounter thought "accidentally" intersecting our minds.

So **the third key to hearing God's voice is recognizing that God's voice in your heart often sounds like a flow of spontaneous thoughts.** Therefore, when I want to hear from God, I tune to chance-encounter or spontaneous thoughts.

Finally, God told Habakkuk to record the vision (Hab. 2:2). This was not an isolated command. The Scriptures record many examples of individual's prayers and God's replies, such as the Psalms, many of the prophets, and Revelation. I have found that obeying this final principle amplified my confidence in my ability to hear God's voice so that I could finally make living out of His initiatives a way of life. The **fourth key, two-way journaling or the writing out of your prayers and God's answers, brings great freedom in hearing God's voice.**

I have found two-way journaling to be a fabulous catalyst for clearly discerning God's inner, spontaneous flow, because as I journal I am able to write in faith for long periods of time, simply believing it is God.

I know that what I believe I have received from God must be tested. However, testing involves doubt and doubt blocks divine communication, so I do not want to test while I am trying to receive. (See James 1:5-8.) With journaling, I can receive in faith, knowing that when the flow has ended I can test and examine it carefully.

So I wrote down what I believed He had said: "She is insecure."

But the Lord wasn't done. I continued to write the spontaneous thoughts that came to me: "Love her unconditionally. She is flesh of your flesh and bone of your bone."

My mind immediately objected: She is not flesh of my flesh. She is not related to me at all – she is a foster child, just living in my home temporarily. It was definitely time to test this "word from the Lord"!

There are three possible sources of thoughts in our minds: ourselves, satan and the Holy Spirit. It was obvious that the words in my journal did not come from my own mind – I certainly didn't see her as insecure *or* flesh of my flesh. And I sincerely doubted that satan would encourage me to love anyone unconditionally!

Okay, it was starting to look like I might have actually received counsel from the Lord. It was consistent with the names and character of God as revealed in the Scripture, and totally contrary to the names and character of the enemy. So that meant that I was hearing from the Lord, and He wanted me to see the situation in a different light. Rachel was my daughter – part of my family not by blood but by the hand of God Himself. The chaos of her birth home had created deep insecurity about her worthiness to be loved by anyone, including me and including God. Only the unconditional love of the Lord expressed through an imperfect human would reach her heart.

But there was still one more test I needed to perform before I would have absolute confidence that this was truly God's word to me: I needed confirmation from someone else whose spiritual discernment I trusted.

So I went to my wife and shared what I had received. I knew if I could get her validation, especially since she was the one most wronged in the situation, then I could say, at least to myself, "Thus sayeth the Lord."

Needless to say, Patti immediately and without question confirmed that the Lord had spoken to me. My entire planned lecture was forgotten. I returned to my office anxious to hear more. As the Lord planted a new, supernatural love for Rachel within me, He showed me what to say and how to say it to not only address the current issue of household responsibility, but the deeper issues of love and acceptance and worthiness.

Rachel and her brother remained as part of our family for another two years, giving us many opportunities to demonstrate and teach about the Father's love, planting spiritual seeds in thirsty soil. We weren't perfect and we didn't solve all of her issues, but because I had learned to listen to the Lord, we were able to avoid creating more brokenness and separation.

The four simple keys that the Lord showed me from Habakkuk have been used by people of all ages, from four to a hundred and four, from every continent, culture and denomination, to break through into intimate two-way conversations with their loving Father and dearest Friend. Omitting any one of the keys will prevent you from receiving all He wants to say to you. The order of the keys is not important, just that you *use them all*. Embracing all four, by faith, can change your life. Simply quiet yourself down, tune to spontaneity, look for vision, and journal. He is waiting to meet you there.

You will be amazed when you journal! Doubt may hinder you at first, but throw it off, reminding yourself that it is a biblical concept, and that God is present, speaking to His children. Relax. When we cease our labors and enter His rest, God is free to flow (Heb. 4:10).

Why not try it for yourself, right now? Sit back comfortably, take out your pen and paper, and smile. Turn your attention toward the Lord in praise and worship, seeking His face. Many people have found the music and visionary prayer called "A Stroll Along the Sea of Galilee" helpful in getting them started. You can listen to it and download it free at www.CWGMinistries.org/Galilee.

After you write your question to Him, become still, fixing your gaze on Jesus. You will suddenly have a very good thought. Don't doubt it; simply write it down. Later, as you read your journaling, you, too, will be blessed to discover that you are indeed dialoguing with God. If you wonder if it is really the Lord speaking to you, share it with your spouse or a friend. Their input will encourage your faith and strengthen your commitment to spend time getting to know the Lover of your soul more intimately than you ever dreamed possible.

IS IT *REALLY* GOD?

Five ways to be sure what you're hearing is from Him:

1. Test the Origin (1 Jn. 4:1) Thoughts from our own minds are progressive, with one thought leading to the next, however tangentially. Thoughts from the spirit world are spontaneous. The Hebrew word for true prophecy is naba, which literally means to bubble up, whereas false prophecy is ziyd meaning to boil up. True words from the Lord will bubble up from our innermost being; we don't need to cook them up ourselves.

2. Compare It to Biblical Principles God will never say something to you personally which is contrary to His universal revelation as expressed in the Scriptures. If the Bible clearly states that something is a sin, no amount of journaling can make it right. Much of what you journal about will not be specifically addressed in the Bible, however, so an understanding of biblical principles is also needed.

3. Compare It to the Names and Character of God as Revealed in the Bible Anything God says to you will be in harmony with His essential nature. Journaling will help you get to know God personally, but knowing what the Bible says about Him will help you discern what words are from Him. Make sure the tenor of your journaling lines up with the character of God as described in the names of the Father, Son and Holy Spirit.

4. Test the Fruit (Matt. 7:15-20)   What effect does what you are hearing have on your soul and your spirit? Words from the Lord will quicken your faith and increase your love, peace and joy. They will stimulate a sense of humility within you as you become more aware of Who God is and who you are. On the other hand, any words you receive which cause you to fear or doubt, which bring you into confusion or anxiety, or which stroke your ego (especially if you hear something that is "just for you alone – no one else is worthy") must be immediately rebuked and rejected as lies of the enemy.

5. Share It with Your Spiritual Counselors (Prov. 11:14) We are members of a Body! A cord of three strands is not easily broken and God's intention has always been for us to grow together. Nothing will increase your faith in your ability to hear from God like having it confirmed by two or three other people! Share it with your spouse, your parents, your friends, your elder, your group leader, even your grown children can be your sounding board. They don't need to be perfect or super-spiritual; they just need to love you, be committed to being available to you, have a solid biblical orientation, and most importantly, they must also willingly and easily receive counsel. Avoid the authoritarian who insists that because of their standing in the church or with God, they no longer need to listen to others. Find two or three people and let them confirm that you are hearing from God!

Dr. Mark Virkler
Co-Author with Patti Virkler - *4 Keys to Hearing God's Voice*
President – Communion With God Ministries
www.CWGministries.org

◖ You Can Learn To Hear God ◗

You can learn to hear God speak to you. He is talking all the time. He has probably been speaking to you your entire life. When people first learn to hear God's voice they often relate that they have heard God before many times, but didn't know it was God speaking to them. He can speak today in any way that He spoke in the Bible; He hasn't limited Himself to certain ways of speaking.

There are many signs and wonders happening today that we fail to recognize. When are we going to wake up and realize that we are spiritual beings having a temporary physical experience? The natural phenomena around us are not arbitrary. God is always working.

Most people today have little or no understanding that they are primarily spiritual beings. God created us body, soul, and spirit. There are hundreds of passages that mention our human spirit in the Bible and yet, take a survey of your friends or your church. Ask the question, "Have you ever heard teaching about your 'human spirit?'" Most of the time not one person will raise their hand. There are more passages about your human spirit than about the Holy Spirit. Hard to believe? Just look up the word spirit and read every passage in the Bible. You will find that a lot of the time it's talking about our human spirit.

God is spirit, and He talks to our spirit, but we are so unaware of our spirit most of the time. When God speaks to us apart from the Word of God, it's often to our spirit. Our mind often interprets what is in our spirit, so sometimes we receive a message from God in our spirit and then we process that message in our mind and it can sound like our own thoughts. Most of my life I thought that hearing God would sound like the movies and TV where there is thunder rolling in the background and something like the voice of James Earl Jones, or Morgan Freeman rumbles in a deep base, "This is GAAWWDDDD." When I would ask God to speak to me I would have pictures in my mind and thoughts go through my mind. I thought these were distracting me from really hearing God. Little did I know that I was having visions and my mind was interpreting things God was speaking to my spirit.

Jesus modeled for us a relationship with the Father that involved constant communication. We only know of one time where a voice came from heaven and that was at His baptism. Then there was the transfiguration where Moses and Elijah showed up. Yet, Jesus said, "…I do nothing of Myself; but as My Father hath taught Me, I speak these things." John 8:28 (KJ21)

We have a human spirit and God is spirit. It is vital that we learn to be aware of what the Holy Spirit is communicating with our human spirit that God has placed within us.

However, there are dangers involved in hearing God's voice. Throughout time there have been false prophets, false dreams and visions, and lying signs and wonders. Satan himself used scripture to tempt Jesus. There is not one way of God's speaking that the enemy hasn't tried to copy and twist. Does that mean we stop trying to hear God's voice? Absolutely not.

Hearing God is like class 101 with Jesus. His sheep hear his voice. We must hear His voice if we want to follow the shepherd. In order to hear His voice it's important to be still and listen. I've heard God's voice in a room where the music was so loud, you couldn't hear yourself when you yelled. The still small voice was able to penetrate the noise without God even raising His voice. Noise can't drown out what our spirit hears and perceives. Paul perceived things in his spirit from the spirit of God. We can too.

HOW TO PRACTICE HEARING GOD

Take 10-20 minutes each day. If you have more time, then feel free to go as long as you want. I encourage you to do this in a quiet place, if possible. God can speak to us over the noises of life, but for this time frame, seek out a quiet place and time, if possible. As you listen, write everything down that goes through your mind and every image that comes into your head.

While you are listening don't censor what you write down. At the end of your time, ask God for discernment between what He is speaking and what is just your imagination, or daydreaming, or even demonic. Don't worry about making mistakes or getting this wrong. You are not writing something to add to the Bible. Consider this a time of learning.

Be sure to read the Bible every day, and to check anything you believe God might be speaking to you with God's Word at the end of your time of listening.

Pay attention to any pictures that come to your mind. Whether they are moving images or vistas, write down every detail. They may be just colors or objects. Write down all the description you can of what you see. These are likely visions and have meaning that you can later ask God or even other believers to help you interpret. Don't get hung up in the moment on the meaning unless it comes to you.

If a song comes to mind, sing it (to yourself unless you are alone) and pay attention to the words. God may speak through a song. If a scripture reference comes to your mind write it down and look it up after your time of listening, unless you are prompted to look it up right away.

Pay attention to what is happening in your spirit. Are you feeling peaceful or disturbed? What else are you feeling? Ask God to help you with this. He usually speaks to our spirit, but we have such little awareness of our spirit, that we process things mostly in our minds. From the beginning seek to be aware of your spirit and write down what comes to you.

Whatever God asks you to do, if you are certain it is God, then obey Him. He might ask you to stop a habit, break off a relationship that is wrong, stop watching a TV show, or He might ask you to share your faith with someone, or speak a word of encouragement to a total stranger. If you are listening, and you obey it will bless both of you. If you want to keep hearing him, I encourage you to obey Him.

Now, just listen!

Richard Mull
Operation Light Force
OperationLightForce@gmail.com
www.GodSpeaksBible.com or
www.OperationLightForce.com

Cover and Interior Design:
Jeff Damm Design, LLC

Editor:
Marlin Birkey

Printed in the United States of America
First Printing, 2015

ISBN
978-0692570739

JESSE BIRKEY
PO Box 816
Riverview, FL 33568
www.jessebirkey.com

This page intentionally left blank

January

Behold, I am doing a new thing! Now it springs forth; do you not perceive and know it and will you not give heed to it? I will even make a way in the wilderness and rivers in the desert.

– ISAIAH 43:19

January 1

MY VOICE WILL BECOME CLEARER AND CLEARER.

I am making a way for you in the desert where there looks to be no way. You will have everything you need. I will encounter you in new ways, and will continue to cover your wounds in order to bring healing. Mountains will crumble before you. I will show you that I am the one who breaks through obstacles, and am able to give you the same breaker anointing.

You will see the beauty of my heart in new ways. Fresh revelations and outpourings of my love will overwhelm you. I will not forsake you. Never! Do not lose sight of my holy mountain, for there is safety and wisdom within. Pursue me with all of your heart.

I will exalt your name and bring you opportunities for advancement. Wait for me to clear the road. Do not move forward until I give the okay to do so. The schemes against you are constant, but I have overcome. I am your general and your captain. Seek my guidance and direction.

Behold, I am doing a new thing! Now it springs forth; do you not perceive and know it and will you not give heed to it? I will even make a way in the wilderness and rivers in the desert.

– ISAIAH 43:19

January 2

I AM POURING MY WATER INTO THE EARTH, and life springs up everywhere. Loving kindness and tenderness cause things to grow and flourish. But harsh words cause wilting and regression. Watch your words. They will begin to carry more weight and anointing. I am doing this. I am making them more powerful. Know this and seek wisdom. Pursue my heart and it will go well.

I am digging a deep well in your life. It is a well that runs deep in me. The water that comes forth is life. It is not just for you, but for others as well. I will put you in positions to share that water with many others. You will see them refreshed in my goodness and love, which will transform them in ways they have never experienced. This is not normal water; it springs forth from a relationship of intimacy and trust. As our relationship grows, I will give you more responsibility and influence.

But whoever takes a drink of the water that I will give him shall never, no never, be thirsty any more. But the water that I will give him shall become a spring of water welling up (flowing, bubbling) [continually] within him unto (into, for) eternal life.
– JOHN 4:14

January 3

REST IN MY LOVE. Your answers are waiting there. I will whisper them to you, so listen for my voice. I love what you do. Let me pour into you, and I will flow through you. I will put my words on your heart.

The drive for perfection is flawed at its core. It is a set up for failure and discouragement. It simply cannot be achieved. Perfection is a myth. It continually moves higher than you can reach. Perfection is an ideal that is unattainable.

But here is the thing: I call you, and the things you do, beautiful. I give them life and worth. I love them. I want you to keep going. You are doing great, but detach your sense of personal worth from what you do. It is not there. Even excellent performance does not have the ability to give you the life you need. Only I can give you that. Let me pour life into your heart so you can be filled to overflowing. Rest in me, and you will find life.

Keep me as the apple of your eye; hide me in the shadow of your wings.
                    – PSALM 17:8

January 4

I LOVE YOU, AND YOU MAKE ME SMILE. The sound of your laughter is sweet to my ears. Let the work of your hands proclaim my name. Let the words of your mouth honor me. Let my love fill your heart and compel you to express it freely.

Be slow to speak, slow to anger, and quick to forgive. Become unoffendable. I am protecting your heart, and it is secure in me. It is no longer you who live, but I who live though you. Let my life become yours.

You are a butterfly emerging from the cocoon, ready to be revealed to the world. Let the world watch us dance together.

Understand [this], my beloved brethren. Let every man be quick to hear [a ready listener], slow to speak, slow to take offense and to get angry.

– JAMES 1:19

January 5

MY SPIRIT IS RUSHING, SWIRLING, AND FILLING.
Get caught up in it and be filled to overflowing. Dance, rejoice, and be glad, for I have come. Victory is mine, and it shall be known.

You are free, so be free in me. I am the ocean of LIFE that the thirsty pursue to receive refreshment. I am the wave of love that knocks down, no, *destroys*, all obstacles. I am peace, love, and joy. Know me, and know my heart.

I am everlasting LIFE. Come to the foot of my stool, and let me see your face. You are so precious to me. You are so desperately loved and cared for. Seek revelation, and open up your heart. I am sending, and have sent, wisdom to you.

And I saw the glory of the God of Israel coming from the east. His voice was like the roar of rushing waters, and the land was radiant with his glory.

– EZEKIEL 43:2

January 6

I HAVE A PLACE FOR YOU. I have heard your prayers. Trust me and believe that I know what you need. I will provide. I will bring LIFE even to the places you think are dead. There is nowhere I step that does not burst with LIFE. My touch brings lasting change.

You are a vessel filled with my blood. Let it pour out of you in order to cleanse, heal, and set the captives free. Let it wash away any stains and usher in abundant LIFE.

Do not look to the left or right, but keep your eyes on me. Get ready. An adventure is coming. This is your life. This is your life in me. It is satisfying and fulfilling.

And He said to me, "Son of man, can these bones live?" And I answered, "O Lord God, You know." Again He said to me, "Prophesy to these bones and say to them, 'O dry bones, hear the word of the Lord.' Thus says the Lord God to these bones, 'Behold, I will make breath enter you so that you may come to life. I will put sinews on you, make flesh grow back on you, cover you with skin, and I will put breath in you so that you may come alive; and you will know that I am the Lord.

– EZEKIEL 37:3-6

❧ *January 7* ❧

I HAVE WON. I AM VICTORIOUS over darkness; it shall never defeat light. I love you. You are so precious to me, and I love just looking at you. I have fashioned you after my own heart. I have filled you with love, peace, and gentleness. These are just *some* of the things I have placed in your heart. Let them become normal for you in a world where they can seem so abnormal.

I am revealing myself to you in different stages according to your ability to receive. I will not pour a measure of wine into a wineskin that has not been prepared to hold it. As I add the wine, little by little, the skin will stretch and be capable of holding even more.

Seek wisdom. Love her, and invite her to grow. She will be a sweet fragrance to you if you allow her into your heart.

Neither is new wine put in old wineskins; for if it is, the skins burst and are torn in pieces, and the wine is spilled and the skins are ruined. But new wine is put into fresh wineskins, and so both are preserved.

– MATTHEW 9:17

January 8

I AM YOUR SOLID FOUNDATION. Nothing else will uphold you. Nothing else will uphold you. Nothing else will bring solid ground underneath your feet. I am your rock, and I will not be moved. I am *for* you. My hand goes before you to make a way. I draw my sword and walk in front of you. I am also your shield. Wait and see how I create the possible from the impossible and the supernatural from the natural.

Let my water flow forth and drown all iniquity. You can drink from my water without fear or concern that it will sweep you away. It carries LIFE, and I am preparing you to be a vessel for that water. When you release it, those around you will be soaked.

Do not rely on what you can see with your natural eye because there is so much going on that you *cannot* see. Be sensitive to my leadings and I will let you know the best way to proceed.

Therefore with joy will you draw water from the wells of salvation.
– ISAIAH 12:3

But Jesus looked at them and said, "With men this is impossible, but all things are possible with God."
– MATTHEW 19:26

January 9

I LOVE YOU. EMBRACE THE SPIRIT of rest that is with you now. There is no agenda. Just be with me and receive.

I am a fountain, a never ending well that bubbles up from the ground. I am like the seasons: always moving and changing. But my character remains the same. Move with me. Trust me enough to step forward, and I will prepare the road to meet your feet. Open your eyes to see what I am doing in you and around you. There is no sweeter place for you than in my arms.

What is the sweetest place you can imagine? I created it. The creator is far better than even the creation. I have colors and effects you have never seen or imagined; open the door of your dreams, and I will show them to you.

One thing have I asked of the Lord, that will I seek, inquire for, and [insistently] require: that I may dwell in the house of the Lord [in His presence] all the days of my life, to behold and gaze upon the beauty [the sweet attractiveness and the delightful loveliness] of the Lord and to meditate, consider, and inquire in His temple.

– PSALM 27:4

January 10

I LOVE YOU. YOU ARE PRECIOUS TO ME. Exalt me in your life and I will exalt you at the appointed time. Persevere with unbreakable faith. I will begin to show you more. I will expose more in you because I want to continue changing you into my image.

My goals and purposes for you will become clearer as we move forward. Trust me and let me lead you. Remember that there is nothing in this world that is the *missing piece* for you. It is my spirit alone that propels you forward. I am actively working, though you cannot yet see the result. I want you to succeed! I will break down the walls around you and set you free!

The Breaker [the Messiah] will go up before them. They will break through, pass in through the gate and go out through it, and their King will pass on before them, the Lord at their head.

– MICAH 2:13

And all of us, as with unveiled face, [because we] continued to behold [in the Word of God] as in a mirror the glory of the Lord, are constantly being transfigured into His very own image in ever increasing splendor and from one degree of glory to another; [for this comes] from the Lord [Who is] the Spirit.

– 2 CORINTHIANS 3:18

❧[*January 11*]☙

LET OTHERS KNOW WHAT I HAVE DONE in your life. Be a sharer of my word. Release my word to do its work in the fields, and I will cause the seeds to sprout. I am the Great Gardener. Come alongside of me and I will show you how to nurture a small plant so it can mature and produce fruit. I will do the same in you. I *have* done it in you.

I love you so much. Your cries do not fall on deaf ears. I am a strong fortress for you. Run to me and find shelter. I am truth and LIFE. I am the answer for your groaning. I have come to restore order, and order there shall be. I have come to restore peace, and peace there shall be.

My glory is all around you. It is raining on you. Be consumed by it.

I am the true vine, and my Father is the gardener. He cuts off every branch in me that bears no fruit, while every branch that does bear fruit he prunes so that it will be even more fruitful.

– JOHN 15 1-2

January 12

I AM WITH YOU. I ALWAYS WILL BE, and I always have been. Drink of me and be glad. I rejoice in your rejoicing. There is a flood coming, a flood of my spirit. It will cover everything. You will know me in ways you have not before.

I just love. I know no other way. Love is who I am. I cannot contain it. It bursts forth and brings LIFE everywhere it goes. It makes the fields ready for harvest. It brings light to the darkness. It sets captives free. There is no other way to be free than to be rescued by my love. It is the greatest story ever told. Let it be your story.

You have ravished my heart and given me courage, my sister, my [promised] bride; you have ravished my heart and given me courage with one look from your eyes, with one jewel of your necklace.
– SONG OF SOLOMON 4:9

January 13

I AM WITH YOU, AND I WILL ALWAYS PROVIDE what you need in every season of your life. When the path is bumpy, I will fit you with shoes equipped to handle the terrain. When the path is steep, I will fit you with gear to make the climb. When the path is easy and peaceful, I will walk leisurely with you.

No matter what, I will be there to guide you and hold your hand. Forget about the next step and just enjoy the journey. Again, I will be with you. Trust me when I say I have good plans for you!

Now may the God of peace [the source of serenity and spiritual well-being] who brought up from the dead our Lord Jesus, the great Shepherd of the sheep, through the blood that sealed and ratified the eternal covenant, equip you with every good thing to carry out His will and strengthen you [making you complete and perfect as you ought to be], accomplishing in us that which is pleasing in His sight, through Jesus Christ, to whom be the glory forever and ever. Amen.

– HEBREWS 13:20-21

January 14

AMIDST THE CRAZINESS, I AM HERE bringing peace like in the eye of a storm. If you will seek me in that moment of chaos, I will guide you through it peacefully, and the storm will dissipate around you.

In each and every situation, I have a perfect solution for you. Look for me in those moments. It blesses me when you invite me in and share your heart, and even your frustrations, with me. I am always available to you.

"For the mountains may be removed and the hills may shake, but My loving kindness will not be removed from you, nor will My covenant of peace be shaken," says the Lord who has compassion on you.

– ISAIAH 54:10

And He got up and [sternly] rebuked the wind and said to the sea, "Hush, be still (muzzled)!" And the wind died down [as if it had grown weary] and there was [at once] a great calm [a perfect peacefulness].

– ISAIAH 43:19

❧[*January 15*]❧

I HAVE YOU ON A COURSE. Stay with me. Rest in me. I have my arms around you, and I do not ever want you to leave. I promise I will not.

Search out wisdom like it is a rare treasure to be found. I will show you the way, and I will show you the truth.

I have clothed you with righteousness and honor. I am so proud of you. You make me smile. I love you, and I love your passion. Use it for my kingdom. The enemy seeks to use your passion to destroy, but I will use it to bring LIFE.

Follow me. I am your shepherd. Look to me, not to others. I am the way, the truth, and the life. Come to me and you will be filled.

Little children, you are of God [you belong to Him] and have [already] defeated and overcome them [the agents of the antichrist], because He who lives in you is greater (mightier) than he who is in the world.

– 1 JOHN 4:4

January 16

SEEK ME, AND YOU WILL FIND ME. I am not hiding from you, but you must open your eyes if you want to see me.

I am going to use you in order to touch hearts and renew minds. We will do it together. Do not be discouraged at the things happening around you. Just watch and see. Be inspired and excited. Let your spirit rise.

I have given you a new cloak – a robe of bright and glorious colors. My glory reflects and bounces off the jewels embedded in it.

I love you so much, and I will never leave you. You will never be forsaken. Be my hands and feet. Pray with confidence in my character. Be sensitive to my leadings. Your words will be like honey because they come from my heart. I am preparing hearts around you to receive.

I will greatly rejoice in the Lord, my soul will exult in my God; for He has clothed me with the garments of salvation, He has covered me with the robe of righteousness, as a bridegroom decks himself with a garland, and as a bride adorns herself with her jewels.

– ISAIAH 61:10

❦ *January 17* ❧

MY LOVE FOR YOU IS EXPLOSIVE! It is more powerful than any other force. I have blessed and empowered you in so many ways. Everything I do is driven by my love for you. If I did not love, the earth would cease to exist like stars that fall from the sky and fizzle out.

You have LIFE because of my great love for you. When you are walking with me, you not only have LIFE, but abundant LIFE! The many gifts I have given you are for the purpose of living out this abundant LIFE. I am grieved when my children squander their gifts and miss out on my best. Will you take my hand and passionately live your destiny?

The thief comes only in order to steal and kill and destroy. I came that they may have and enjoy life, and have it in abundance [to the full, till it overflows].
– JOHN 10:10

"My beloved speaks and says to me, 'Arise, my love, my fair one, and come away.'
– SONG OF SOLOMON 2:10

January 18

FOCUSING ON THE HERE AND NOW. There are times when I will give you glimpses of what I have planned for you in the future, but I am calling you to focus on one step at a time. Tomorrow has enough worries. I will provide your daily bread, as I always have. Choose to trust me in each and every step. For now, lay aside the questions about tomorrow and rest in me.

I will walk with you through every single step. When you move ahead of me while fixing your eyes in the distance, you will stumble over the next place to set your foot. Walk hand in hand with me and I will guide you over and around these unnecessary stumbling stones.

Therefore do not worry about tomorrow, for tomorrow will worry about itself. Each day has enough trouble of its own.
– MATTHEW 6:34

He will not let your foot slip; he who watches over you will not slumber.
– PSALM 121:3

{ January 19 }

MANY TIMES BUSYNESS IS A LIE. There are plenty of hours in the day, and there is always time for you and me. Come to me when you are burdened and heavy laden, and I will give you rest. I will take your troubles and cares and give you my yoke, which is light and easy.

You are like a loaf of bread baking in a warm oven. I am the oven and you are becoming what you were created to be. I have placed guards around you to watch over and protect you. What do you need? Ask me for it. What is on your heart? Tell me about it.

I want you to be compelled by my love. It is a love that cannot be stopped. It advances like fire and consumes the darkness that aims to cover you. It is alive and active in you and through you.

For the Word that God speaks is alive and full of power [making it active, operative, energizing, and effective]; it is sharper than any two-edged sword, penetrating to the dividing line of the breath of life (soul) and [the immortal] spirit, and of joints and marrow [of the deepest parts of our nature], exposing and sifting and analyzing and judging the very thoughts and purposes of the heart.

– HEBREWS 4:12

January 20

LOOK! THE CLOUDS ARE PARTING and the sun is shining. The rays are reaching out and filling everyone they touch with joy. Dance in my glory.

Great things are coming, child. Do not miss them by focusing your eyes on things that are not of me. I delight in your laughter. I invite you to live as freely as a child twirling in the rain. Do not let the darkness consume you. Tell it to flee, and dive into my light!

He called a little child and set him before them, and said, "I assure you and most solemnly say to you, unless you repent [that is, change your inner self—your old way of thinking, live changed lives] and become like children [trusting, humble, and forgiving], you will never enter the kingdom of heaven. Therefore, whoever humbles himself like this child is greatest in the kingdom of heaven.

– MATTHEW 18:2-4

Let them praise His name with dancing; let them sing praises to Him with the tambourine and lyre.

– PSALM 149:3

January 21

I LOVE YOU. YOU ARE THE LIGHT of my eyes and I am so very proud of you. My life pours into you as we walk and talk. Come and rest with me in our spot. Just be with me now. There is no pressure or agenda here. Just be. Invest yourself in this moment.

Feel my arms around you as I squeeze you tight. I will never let you go. My breath is sweet and your fragrance tickles my nose. I never leave this place. I AM this place. You are in me, so you share in this place. Yield to the peace that exists here.

My presence is why you can have peace in any circumstance. It is not somewhere you go, it is something you welcome into each moment. You carry it with you wherever you go because it is me. You are in it right now, and you will be in it later. The only thing that changes is your awareness.

You will guard him and keep him in perfect and constant peace whose mind [both its inclination and its character] is stayed on You, because he commits himself to You, leans on You, and hopes confidently in You.

– ISAIAH 26:3

January 22

I AM GIVING YOU MY EYES so that you can see yourself as I see you: lovely, holy, pure, loved, adored, highly valued, highly significant, and so much more!

I also want you to look differently at the things around you, things like homes, nature, and work. Do not forget that where my presence is, there is beauty and freedom. Look past the surface and see me in everything around you.

I do not need you to *perform*. The drive to perform will force you into someone you are not. I just want you to be yourself. Be who I have made you to be. Let the pressure float away.

Oh child, the things you desire are in my hands. All I have to do is open my hands. But be patient because I am waiting for the right time. Trust me in the walk and in the process. We have to do this together. I know the desires of your heart and I am working to make them a reality.

Delight yourself also in the Lord, and He will give you the desires and secret petitions of your heart.

– PSALM 37:4

January 23

I HAVE SO MUCH JOY AND LOVE I want to give you and pour through you. You are so awesome. I love you, and I am your lamp. Set your eyes on me and hold my hands. Step on my feet like a child dances with its father, and we will go together.

You are a big deal to me. Let me cover you like a blanket. This is what I desire – to love you and to be with you.

I have set up a place for us at the top of the mountain. Some have every tool under the sun to try and climb up the mountain. Strip it all off and just walk forward. Leave everything you thought would help at the foot of the mountain. The steps are easy and the burden is light.

I want you to be prepared when you go out into the world. Intimate relationship with me is where you learn how to work the ground in a way that produces good fruit. Do not be caught unprepared. Do not allow pride to invite the enemy to take you by surprise.

Who may ascend onto the mountain of the Lord? And who may stand in His holy place? He who has clean hands and a pure heart, who has not lifted up his soul to what is false, nor has sworn [oaths] deceitfully.

– PSALM 24:3-4

{ *January 24* }

OH, THE FOUNTAINS THAT FEED MY LOVE for you are so deep and wide. The pool from where my love flows literally has no bottom. You can swim down forever only to discover more depth and increasing revelation. I invite you to swim, splash, and play.

Limits are built into how you understand the world. The spiritual operates under different parameters and boundaries. Some things are too wonderful for you right now. They are like a speeding train with so much brilliant light that it overwhelms your senses. I will show you these things in time, but it will be when you are best prepared to see the beauty of them.

You have already seen so much of my beauty. You reflect it to others without even realizing it. You carry my intimate heart. Carry it like a prize possession. Show it off like a trophy.

O give thanks to the God of heaven, for His mercy and loving kindness endure forever! .

– PSALM 136:26

January 25

I LOVE YOU. I AM CONSUMING YOU from the inside out. My love is a wave inside of you, breaking down everything standing in its way. It is breaking free from the depths and rising up. Steward it. Be a steward of my love inside of you, for as it changes you it will change others.

Do not forget about, or minimize, holiness – it is very important to me. I stand on a mountain and call my children to chase my heart. The invitation is costly; it often costs something you hold dear, even your treasure.

But it is LIFE I invite you into. Your treasure is death, but mine is LIFE, and I offer it freely. Those who feel forsaken are those who have refused the treasure I have made available to them. They have decided to hold other things much closer to their hearts.

For where your treasure is, there will your heart be also.

– MATTHEW 6:2

January 26

LEAVE THE DEAD TO THE DEAD because LIFE is before you. Set your eyes on the things above, not those dying below. This is where the power of sin is broken. This is where evil is undone. As you fall into me, you fall out of the world. As you step into me, you step into LIFE.

In me is the fullest measure of peace. In me is love everlasting. Cut yourself loose from the anchors holding you fast to the world and sink deeper into my presence than you ever have. Let my waves of love cover you.

I am the river of LIFE. If you drink from me, the insatiable thirst of your heart will be quenched and the joy you desire will be released. There is an outpouring of joy coming soon. I am coming to those who have felt the heavy burden of oppression for a long time. I am coming to show them the light and the way to me.

You will show me the path of life; in Your presence is fullness of joy, at Your right hand there are pleasures forevermore.

– PSALM 16:11

January 27

ARISE, MY CHILD. WALK CONFIDENTLY in your calling. I will lead the blind along unfamiliar ways. I have never abandoned you, and I never will. Your calling is not the same as others, for it is specifically designed for you. I will grow you as you are obedient with each new opportunity I provide.

The Holy Spirit will guide your words in all assignments. Keep a watch at your mouth. Let your words be my words. Let your voice be my voice. I will put a new song in your mouth. Sing praises, sing praises, sing praises! Continue to rest in me in all things.

"I will lead the blind by a way they do not know; I will guide them in paths that they do not know. I will make darkness into light before them and rugged places into plains. These things I will do [for them], and I will not leave them abandoned or undone."

– ISAIAH 42:16

He put a new song in my mouth, a song of praise to our God; many will see and fear [with great reverence] and will trust confidently in the Lord.

– PSALM 40:3

January 28

FOLLOW ME. JUST FOLLOW ME and be led by my spirit. Do not be afraid to hope for greatness. Choose belief. Know that I am able to do great and mighty things. Share in my greatness.

My kingdom is often like a pathway of pavers that light up one by one with each step you take. Let me light the steps for you. In order for the pavers to light up, you must take a step. The paver will not light up until your foot lands. It is my desire that these steps would be full of faith and excitement, not fear and trepidation!

'Call to Me and I will answer you, and tell you [and even show you] great and mighty things, [things which have been confined and hidden], which you do not know and understand and cannot distinguish.

– JEREMIAH 33:3

Your word is a lamp to my feet and a light to my path.

– PSALM 119:105

YOU ARE INSPIRING. KEEP DANCING WITH ME.
Learn how to flow and rest with me. Let your heart be known, and let compassion lead you. Hear my voice and know me. Dive into my goodness. I am light. There is no darkness in me at all.

Look for others to honor and lift up. Let jealousy and envy be far from you. You cannot increase your standing with me because you are already my favorite. There is nothing you could ever do to make me love you any more, or any less. Do not take on any condemnation or guilt. Those are not coming from me.

And this is the message [the message of promise] which we have heard from Him and now are reporting to you: God is Light, and there is no darkness in Him at all [no, not in any way].

– 1 JOHN 1:5

For wherever there is jealousy (envy) and contention (rivalry and selfish ambition), there will also be confusion (unrest, disharmony, rebellion) and all sorts of evil and vile practices.

– JAMES 3:16

January 30

I AM RELENTLESS AGAINST HARD GROUND. But that first layer can be very thick depending on the things you have experienced and what you believe to be true. However, what is hard can be broken in a moment. If I can break through the outer layer, the soil is soft.

Love is the softener. Self-sacrificial love is the only thing that can breech the hard outer layer and penetrate down to the rich soil. Love is who I am. Let it be who you are, also. If you do, every step you take will leave a soft, but life-changing, impression.

Allow my love to pour down into the depths of who you are. I long to know and lead you on the path I have marked out for you. I will not be careless or flippant with your love. It is the most precious thing to me. It is okay to trust me with yourself. Let's swim together in the ocean of my goodness where spouts of praise burst into the sky.

For the word of the Lord is right; and all His work is done in faithfulness. He loves righteousness and justice; the earth is full of the loving kindness of the Lord. By the word of the Lord were the heavens made, and all their host by the breath of His mouth.

– PSALM 33:4-6

January 31

LET ME SING OVER YOU WHILE YOU REST in my sweet presence. I will bring rest and joy to your soul. I am the only one who can do that for you. Pursue my peace and it will fill you to overflowing. I have made a place for you in my heart. Do not forget to laugh and have fun; I am fun; I am LIFE. Be a child. Allow yourself to feel like one in my arms.

I am showing you things, even greater things. Take hold of the courage I have offered. Faith will lead you forward, not back to the past. Trust in me, not in what you can see. The glory of what I am building today will outshine anything you have experienced so far.

I will open your eyes to see the inner workings of hearts around you. I have placed tools in your hands to help them. This is an assignment with a high calling. If you let me, I will surround you with a community who can help you.

Brothers and sisters, I do not consider that I have made it my own yet; but one thing I do: forgetting what lies behind and reaching forward to what lies ahead, I press on toward the goal to win the [heavenly] prize of the upward call of God in Christ Jesus.
– PHILIPPIANS 3:13-14

February

Show me Your ways, O Lord; teach me
Your paths. Guide me in Your truth
and faithfulness and teach me, for You
are the God of my salvation; for You
[You only and altogether] do I wait
[expectantly] all the day long.

– PSALM 25:4-5

February 1

I LOVE YOU. BREATHE AND SWAY WITH ME. You are a mighty warrior. You have questioned your intelligence and ability to strategize and organize. No more! Your input is valuable. Do not hesitate to speak up. Let your voice be heard. It is my wisdom that pours through you. It is my wisdom that sparks LIFE in your bones and heart.

Purpose for you has been birthed from my heart. I will pour out purpose, hope, and vision into your heart and mind. But be patient. You can make your own plans, or you can let me guide your steps. Grab onto LIFE and others will follow you.

Be open and soft like a gel capsule rather than being like an acorn. Let there be no resistance to my love pouring out of you. You have taken measures to protect yourself, but many times those measures have kept out what is needed for you to grow. Trust me and the work I am doing in you.

Show me Your ways, O Lord; teach me Your paths. Guide me in Your truth and faithfulness and teach me, for You are the God of my salvation; for You [You only and altogether] do I wait [expectantly] all the day long.

–PSALM 25:4-5

February 2

I LOVE YOU. DO NOT LOOK AT HOW I encounter others to decide how I should be encountering you. The ways I encounter you are just as powerful. Stop comparing yourself to others.

Come! Taste and see that I am good. Come and find your LIFE. I stand at the door and knock. Will you open it to me? Give me the keys to your heart. Let me direct and guide your steps. I will lead you to glory, never to destruction.

I love you so much. You are so precious to me. Never forget how I feel about you. I long for you like a traveler in the desert longs for water. You are mine and I am yours. Seek and you will find. I have made all things white like snow. You are fresh, undefiled, and pure. I have covered and wiped clean all of the stains you thought you had. There is nothing that can stand against the power of my cleansing blood.

O taste and see that the Lord [our God] is good! Blessed (happy, fortunate, to be envied) is the man who trusts and takes refuge in Him.

– PSALM 34:8

February 3

LOOK AND BEHOLD MY MIGHT. But also take hold of my gentleness. If you want to be like me, you will need to be a servant. You will need to love self-sacrificially. Let love be an uncompromising force in your life.

I am a wellspring of LIFE for you. Drink of me and you will be filled. Continue being filled by me. Share in my LIFE and seek my heart. You have been seared by my love and branded by my loving kindness. You are love because I am love, and I am in you.

When you look in the mirror, I want you to see the beauty that I see. The sparkle you carry brings a smile to my face. I am full of joy when I gaze at you. This love is not too wonderful for you. Everything that I am is for you.

But this is not to be so among you; instead, whoever desires to be great among you must be your servant, and whoever wishes to be most important and first in rank among you must be slave of all. For even the Son of Man came not to have service rendered to Him, but to serve, and to give His life as a ransom for (instead of) many.

– MARK 10:43-45

February 4

MY LOVE FOR YOU IS GREAT and everlasting! Like the waves of the ocean, which continually flow onto shore, my love is consistent but yet ever changing. Some waves are big and some are small. If they were always big, the shore would be continuously wrecked and unusable. If they were always small, there would never be any change.

This does not speak to the size or depth of my love, but only to the ways in which you experience it. For my love is always a mighty and consuming ocean. Bathe in the ocean of my love today.

See what an incredible quality of love the Father has shown to us, that we would [be permitted to] be named and called and counted the children of God! And so we are! For this reason the world does not know us, because it did not know Him.

– 1 JOHN 3:1

February 5

I AM CREATIVE! Beauty has its beginning in me. Seek my heart and I will reveal beauty beyond what you know or could expect. I am here with you. We are one. I am in you and I will never leave. Set your heart on the things above, the things that give and sustain LIFE.

There is so much death in the world, but do not ever think for a moment that I cannot resurrect it all. Be very slow to write people off as lost forever. That notion does not exist to me.

Keep being courageous. I love you and I love the efforts you make. Stay close to my heart so you can hear my soft voice. Do not get ahead of me. Let me make a way for you. *Be* my love, and reach the world by reflecting who I really am. There are many that do not understand.

Healing is what I want. Wholeness is what I long for. I came for *you*. I long for you to know and love me. My heart is so full of desire for you to be buried in my arms. Welcome to the wedding ceremony.

Your eyes will see the King in His beauty; they will see a far-distant land.

– ISAIAH 33:17

February 6

I AM NEVER THE ONE WHO BRINGS SHAME and condemnation to you. That is the enemy working to gain a place in your life. I am of whatever is good, holy, uplifting, and encouraging. I am fresh air in a stale room, a cool breeze in a desert, and a warm apple pie on an autumn day.

Your feet are continually being rooted in my love. I feel your heart beginning to shift. Allow it to happen. Let me move you to a deeper place in me. I want to move through you in power, but I want you to let me decide what that is going to look like. No matter what it looks like, the people around you will be impacted by my presence.

Finally, believers, whatever is true, whatever is honorable and worthy of respect, whatever is right and confirmed by God's word, whatever is pure and wholesome, whatever is lovely and brings peace, whatever is admirable and of good repute; if there is any excellence, if there is anything worthy of praise, think continually on these things [center your mind on them, and implant them in your heart].

– PHILIPPIANS 4:8

February 7

I AM DOING A NEW THING. I have taken you through a winter. Though things have seemed dead and desolate at times, there is LIFE underneath the hard layers. The seeds have only been slumbering, waiting for spring.

My people's hearts are changing, and there is LIFE waiting to break through the cold ground. The spring has come; the hearts of my people are bursting forth like flowers. As this happens, the flowers will produce many seeds that will go forth and find soft, ready soil. New flowers will then begin springing up all around.

I am melting the cold hearts. I am breaking the strongholds. Prepare your heart, for new things are coming!

Therefore if any person is [ingrafted] in Christ (the Messiah) he is a new creation (a new creature altogether); the old [previous moral and spiritual condition] has passed away. Behold, the fresh and new has come!.

– 2 CORINTHIANS 5:17

February 8

I LOVE YOU. YOU ARE SO SPECIAL AND AMAZING.
I smile at you so much more than you know. I stand ready to release my spirit on you. Ask me and I will pour it out. There is so much even beyond what you know to ask for. Seek my heart and open up to even greater things.

Let your light shine before me. Do not be afraid to dance. The level of skill does not matter. I love watching you be free.

I am an open book and the words are for you. I love you. I cherish you. You are mine. My hand will never let you go. I am always watching you, looking for ways to help, and hoping you will ask me to.

So David said to Michal, "It was before the Lord [that I did this], who chose me above your father and all his house, to appoint me as ruler over Israel, the people of the Lord. Therefore I will celebrate [in pure enjoyment] before the Lord. Yet I will demean myself even more than this, and will be humbled (abased) in my own sight [and yours, as I please], but by the maids whom you mentioned, by them I shall be held in honor."

– 2 SAMUEL 21-22

February 9

PICTURE A FIELD FULL OF WILTED FLOWERS.
One breath from my mouth, and all of the petals reach up to the sky. They reach up for me. Just one touch and what is crushed becomes something bursting with LIFE. Eyes fixed on the ground suddenly lift to the heavens. Despair becomes hope. And here I stand day after day, year after year, asking every single one if I can breathe on them, if I can touch them.

Even still they are such a pleasing fragrance to me, even in this state. I can change everything, but they must decide to let me lift their heads. They must say no to the darkness before they can say yes to the light.

I long for abundant LIFE in you. This is what makes my heart rejoice. I will even leave the fields full of thriving flowers to find one that is lost and ready for my touch. I came for the sick, and I am constantly searching them out. This is how I have always pursued you, and it is how I will always pursue you.

"I am the rose [of the plain] of Sharon, The lily of the valleys [that grows in deep places]." "Like the lily among the thorns, So are you, my darling, among the maidens.

– ISAIAH 43:19

February 10

I AM ABLE TO USE ALL THINGS for my purpose and kingdom. I am not concerned with the opinions that come from others. They are nothing in the grand scheme of what I am bringing to fruition in your life. See, I am doing a new thing. My love is being revealed in a new way.

At times, the transitions into the new may have a few bumps, but the fruit will far outweigh the minor struggles. My love will sustain you through any discomfort that may come. I have prepared your heart for this.

For our momentary, light distress [this passing trouble] is producing for us an eternal weight of glory [a fullness] beyond all measure [surpassing all comparisons, a transcendent splendor and an endless blessedness]!

– 2 CORINTHIANS 4:17

And we know [with great confidence] that God [who is deeply concerned about us] causes all things to work together [as a plan] for good for those who love God, to those who are called according to His plan and purpose.

– ROMANS 8:28

February 11

I LOVE YOU SO MUCH, and I make all things new. My spirit is limitless. Rest in me. Lay yourself down and find rest in the shadow of my wings. Your security and peace is here. I am your healer and restorer. This is where the bleeding is stopped and the wounds are healed. I will put the broken pieces back together again.

Embrace the spirit of wisdom and revelation. Let it make its home in you. It is my spirit. I am wisdom and I am revelation. Let my presence rest on you.

Let the outpouring of my love saturate and flood your relationships. My love will be your anchor. When you feel the winds of the storms are too strong, drop your anchor in my love and it will hold you fast. You will be saved.

He will cover you and completely protect you with His pinions, and under His wings you will find refuge; His faithfulness is a shield and a wall.

– PSALM 91:4

February 12

JUST FALL INTO MY ARMS. Ah, this is where you need to be. Your place is in my arms. I love you so much. When you are hungry, I will feed you. If you are thirsty, I will give you something to drink.

Praise the Lord, oh, your soul. All that is within you praise my holy name. For I am LIFE to your lungs, your heart, and your body. There is nothing else that can be the answer for you.

I am a mountain you do not have to climb. In fact, I come down to you. In the fields and in the lilies, I am there. Seek my treasure and you will find it. Do not worry or be afraid. I have got you.

But whoever drinks the water that I give him will never be thirsty again. But the water that I give him will become in him a spring of water [satisfying his thirst for God] welling up [continually flowing, bubbling within him] to eternal life."

– JOHN 4:14

February 13

SPLASH AROUND IN MY GOODNESS. I want to show you greater things. Come into the deeper waters with me. Follow me below the surface.

Hold my hand as we wade through the mysteries. Watch for the steep drop-offs. We are going deeper now. Do not slip on the loose sand. I am right in front of you. Stop holding your breath. You can breathe with me, but you will not be able to if you let go.

And here is the city, my city. It is hidden to the world and requires a walk with me to find it. It is for you and all those who follow me. The mystery does not simply end with the unveiling of the city, but there are many wonders within.

There are rooms upon rooms filled with treasure. Not treasure like you would find on earth, but treasure that will enrich your heart instead of your wallet. For there are no possessions to be bought here, only discovered, and I am the key. I unlock every room. Stay beside me and we will visit every single one.

And I saw the holy city, new Jerusalem, coming down out of heaven from God, arrayed like a bride adorned for her husband;

– REVELATION 21:2

February 14

JUST STEP FORWARD AND FOLLOW ME. It is my great pleasure to unlock my heart for those who truly want it. And I know you do.

I hear the sound of your heart knocking against the places you want to go in me. The door swings wide and you step inside. It is almost too great for you as you now are, but the day is coming, and coming soon, when you shall behold my intense glory and not be overcome, but be filled.

In this world you will have trouble, but take heart; I have overcome the world. I am alive and I have come. Do not let hope slip away. Let joy abound even in the face of trouble. Let joy spark your heart because I am right next to you. Whatever you face, we face together.

Bless those who trouble you. Perceive beyond the darkness and see my fingerprints on everyone, no matter how hidden they might be.

I have told you these things, so that in Me you may have [perfect] peace. In the world you have tribulation and distress and suffering, but be courageous [be confident, be undaunted, be filled with joy]; I have overcome the world." [My conquest is accomplished, My victory abiding.]

– JOHN 16:33

February 15

I AM THE WAY, THE TRUTH, AND THE LIFE. I am the last cup you will ever need. I will fill you to overflowing. I am exalted in front of you because I am the one who saves. If you look to me you will be healed. I will cover all of your blemishes like snow covers the ground.

I am doing surgery inside of your heart. You have asked me for more, and I am making the preparations necessary to allow that to happen. Be patient. I am working in you and through you, even if you do not see it. You are, and will be, an incredible influence for me.

For it is [not your strength, but it is] God who is effectively at work in you, both to will and to work [that is, strengthening, energizing, and creating in you the longing and the ability to fulfill your purpose] for His good pleasure.

– PHILIPPIANS 2:13

❧ *February 16* ❧

I WILL LEAD YOU STEP BY STEP. You do not have to know where you are going; you just have to trust that I do. My footsteps are soft and my invitations are gentle. Though I am soft and gentle, there is strength in me.

My word is strong like the rocks under the earth. It will shake the valley. And all of that power is in you because I am in you. Be still and know that I am God. It is going to be okay.

I am brighter than the sun. The sun is a natural creation and can only warm the outside. But I warm the heart. The natural world around you can only go skin deep, but I go into the depths of who you are. The world you often do not see is more real and impacting than the one you see every moment.

So we look not at the things which are seen, but at the things which are unseen; for the things which are visible are temporal [just brief and fleeting], but the things which are invisible are everlasting and imperishable.

– 2 CORINTHIANS 4:18

February 17

YOU ARE MY CHILD AND I AM SO PROUD OF YOU!
When you make mistakes, my arms are open to you. Feel my embrace and hear my words. *I love you; you are so special.*

Turn and walk with me again. Dust off your feet and remember the truth of my power within you. It is not you who lives, but I who am alive in you. When you use that power, you are victorious. But if you do not use it, you will lose.

Press forward and never backward. What I have for you is greater than what you had in the past. I am taking you from glory to glory. Do not try to go back, try to move forward. The waters in front of you are deeper and richer than the ones behind.

Your ears will hear a word behind you, "This is the way, walk in it," whenever you turn to the right or to the left.

– ISAIAH 30:21

February 18

YOU ARE WHO I SAY YOU ARE! I am raising you up and doing a great work in you. I am not finished with you yet, for I have only just begun. Follow me and I will lead you. I am asking you to press forward even in the moments you want to turn back. Do not be afraid, for goodness flows from me. I will never leave you or forsake you.

Continually seek my face even in the things that seem mundane, for I am there too. I have amazing things to show you, but more than that, I desire for us to grow in relationship. Great and mighty things will flow out of our relationship.

It is the LORD who goes before you; He will be with you. He will not fail you or abandon you. Do not fear or be dismayed.

– DEUTERONOMY 31:8

I am convinced and confident of this very thing, that He who has begun a good work in you will [continue to] perfect and complete it until the day of Christ Jesus [the time of His return]

– PHILIPPIANS 1:6

February 19

I HAVE GIVEN YOU POWER and authority to overcome everything keeping you from moving forward in me. Command the obstacles to be destroyed. In my name, command the locks and blocks to be broken.

When you feel like you are standing in a dark room, just remember that I am already shining bright. The only thing between you and my glory is a shade. Pull it up. Then I will fill the room and expose the things content to hide in darkness. They will be overcome because they cannot stand against the light. If they are exposed, they will be destroyed.

Now the Lord is the Spirit, and where the Spirit of the Lord is, there is liberty [emancipation from bondage, true freedom]..

– 2 CORINTHIANS 3:17

I assure you and most solemnly say to you, whoever says to this mountain, 'Be lifted up and thrown into the sea!' and does not doubt in his heart [in God's unlimited power], but believes that what he says is going to take place, it will be done for him [in accordance with God's will].

– MARK 11:23

February 20

DO NOT BE IN A RUSH. TAKE YOUR TIME. Many have missed opportunities because they were in a hurry.

In your weaknesses I am strong. The praise of man is fickle. Trust in what I have declared over you, for it is sturdy and steadfast.

I am an iron that flattens out wrinkles. Sometimes it feels like pressure, but there is a greater work being done. Follow me like you would if you could physically see me in front of you. You have my life to guide you. You know my will and desires. Let them be *your* will and desires.

Concerning this I pleaded with the Lord three times that it might leave me; but He has said to me, "My grace is sufficient for you [My loving kindness and My mercy are more than enough— always available—regardless of the situation]; for [My] power is being perfected [and is completed and shows itself most effectively] in [your] weakness."

– 2 CORINTHIANS 12:8-9

February 21

I AM THE WAY, THE TRUTH, AND THE LIFE, to all who come. Come to me and I will consume all of the darkness around you. Do not leave your heavy bags on the outside; rather bring them in so they can be consumed by the fire of my love.

There is always joy and peace with me. The pace I have set for you does not determine your allotment of joy and peace. I have released them to you in full. And there is love. It is a love that you are learning. Sometimes it gets twisted, but I am always unraveling it for you.

I am so proud of you.

Even to your old age I am He, and even to your advanced old age I will carry you! I have made you, and I will carry you; be assured I will carry you and I will save you.
        – ISAIAH 46:4

May the God of hope fill you with all joy and peace in believing [through the experience of your faith] that by the power of the Holy Spirit you will abound in hope and overflow with confidence in His promises.
        – ROMANS 15:13

February 22

IN MY PRESENCE IS FULLNESS OF LIGHT. Remain in me and darkness cannot touch you. Not only can it not touch you, but by simply remaining in me, darkness will be destroyed from wherever you go. Picture yourself with rays of light beaming forth all around your body. As you walk, those rays of light will overtake the darkness.

To walk in my light, be continually aware of my presence and communicate with me constantly. I am there regardless, but when you are aware of it, your entire being is empowered to walk in truth and light.

You are the light of [Christ to] the world. A city set on a hill cannot be hidden.

– MATTHEW 5:14

February 23

I LOVE YOU. YOU ARE SO PRECIOUS TO ME. I love to be with you. Hear and receive my words. They are soothing to your soul.

Follow the trail I have marked out for you. There are places on the path that will need to be forged. I have the tools you need to make it through, and I am going ahead of you to prepare the way. Watch out for the thorns that will try to grab and hurt you. Follow me and you will be safe.

Do not try to ride the emotional waves of success and failure. You are a success because you are my beloved. Many times the world will call you a failure when I am calling you a success. Do not allow the world around you to define you. Let my love define you.

Let me know Your ways, O Lord; Teach me Your paths. Guide me in Your truth and teach me, For You are the God of my salvation; For You [and only You] I wait [expectantly] all the day long.

– PSALM 25:4-5

February 24

I WILL LEAD YOU ON THE HIGHWAY OF HOLINESS.
Follow me and you shall not be destroyed. Pursue me with your whole heart. I will never turn away from you. I want you to lead by being led.

Be gentle and humble. Admit your weaknesses; I will help them to become your strengths.

Stop trying to live two steps ahead. Be patient and we will work through issues as they arise. You are my child and I am very pleased with you. Listen for my voice and you will have instructions.

Let my peace reign in you. Let it quiet any raging storms. If you step out of my shadow, you will find yourself in turmoil. Work *with* me and not *against me*. I love you. I find great joy in you. My desire is to see you succeed.

Judging others will take you out of my peace. Resist the temptation to judge and condemn.

A highway will be there, and a roadway; And it will be called the Holy Way. The unclean will not travel on it, but it will be for those who walk on the way [the redeemed]; And fools will not wander on it.

– ISAIAH 35:8

February 25

COME TO ME IN THE WATERS of refreshing and renewal, the place where comfort abounds and love endures. Tell me all of the things filling your heart. Share the good and bad, the joy and sorrow. I am here.

My kingdom is beautiful and when it is represented as such, it draws people to it. You are like a moth fluttering around the light, waiting for the masses to join you. And they will. You have found the light and are a beacon to others.

"Everyone who thirsts, come to the waters; And you who have no money come, buy grain and eat. Come, buy wine and milk without money and without cost [simply accept it as a gift from God]. Why do you spend money for that which is not bread, and your earnings for what does not satisfy? Listen carefully to Me, and eat what is good, and let your soul delight in abundance. Incline your ear [to listen] and come to Me; Hear, so that your soul may live; And I will make an everlasting covenant with you, According to the faithful mercies [promised and] shown to David.

– ISAIAH 55:1-3

February 26

I KNOW YOU AND I LOVE YOU. Let knowing me more be your greatest pursuit. I will take you on a walk through my heart and let you see who I am. I am revealing myself to you.

Never believe that I am being silent in response to your requests. I hear you and I am responding even though you cannot see it. I love you and I care about what you want.

Fellowship with me; I want you to get to know me. I am available for you. I want to be known.

Now this is eternal life: that they may know You, the only true [supreme and sovereign] God, and [in the same manner know] Jesus [as the] Christ whom You have sent.

– JOHN 17:3

The Lord does not delay [as though He were unable to act] and is not slow about His promise, as some count slowness, but is [extraordinarily] patient toward you, not wishing for any to perish but for all to come to repentance.

– 2 PETER 3:9

❦ *February 27* ❧

LET MY LOVE FILL YOUR WHOLE BEING. Do what you can to make peace. Take my love with you wherever you go.

I can wash your clothes and make you clean, but you must come to me. Do not hold onto your dirty rags. Sometimes it is easy to think they are giving you LIFE, but they are killing you instead. The comfort you feel they provide is a false sense of LIFE. I am the blanket that will cover you in your time of need. I will make you warm when the world is cold.

Come to see me.

Now Joshua was clothed with filthy (nauseatingly vile) garments and was standing before the Angel [of the Lord]. He spoke to those who stood before Him, saying, "Remove the filthy garments from him." And He said to Joshua, "See, I have caused your wickedness to be taken away from you, and I will clothe and beautify you with rich robes [of forgiveness]." And I (Zechariah) said, "Let them put a clean turban on his head." So they put a clean turban on his head and clothed him with [rich] garments. And the Angel of the Lord stood by.

– ZECHARIAH 3:3-5

February 28

RELAX IN ME. RELAX IN MY HEART. You do not have to do this alone. I will be with you every step of the way. I will lead you. You have nothing to worry about. I will do the hard work. Just plant seeds and I will water them. We will do this together.

Listen for my direction. I have prepared you for this. Be a shining reflection of my love. You are successful already because you are loved. You do not have anything to prove. Striving for approval will only drain your energy. When you are with me, you shall run and not be weary.

But those who wait for the Lord [who expect, look for, and hope in Him] will gain new strength and renew their power; They will lift up their wings [and rise up close to God] like eagles [rising toward the sun]; They will run and not become weary, They will walk and not grow tired.

– ISAIAH 40:31

February 29

HOW BEAUTIFUL IS MY DWELLING PLACE. That is you, for I dwell in you. You are precious and beautiful; you are a magnificent creation. Put on my eyes and practice seeing in the mirror what I see. Do not think lowly of yourself. Do not come into agreement with the lies of your adversary. You are worthy, deeply loved, and greatly cared for. If you choose to believe the truth, I will make it your reality.

I will stand with you in the middle of a tornado and you will feel nothing but peace. Taste and see that I am good. I am the river of LIFE. Always keep your feet in me. Lie down in me and let the waters of my heart cool any spot fires.

But you are a chosen race, a royal priesthood, a consecrated nation, a [special] people for God's own possession, so that you may proclaim the excellencies [the wonderful deeds and virtues and perfections] of Him who called you out of darkness into His marvelous light.

– 1 PETER 2:9

March

O my love, you are altogether beautiful
and fair. There is no flaw nor blemish
in you!

– SONG OF SOLOMON 4:7

March 1

CONSIDER YOUR HOUSE. The walls are my hands. The door is my heart. The air circulation is my breath. I am all around you no matter where you are. The sky, the grass, and the dirt; I hold it all together.

I see the blood weave through your veins. I can trace it with my finger. I am in all and I am all. And I love you so much. You are my delight. I would get up before dawn to watch you rise like the sun. I would capture all of the instruments in the world to play you the most beautiful song. I would dance with you a dance that never ends. Will you come with me?

O my love, you are altogether beautiful and fair. There is no flaw nor blemish in you!

– SONG OF SOLOMON 4:7

March 2

I HAVE PLANTED SEEDS IN YOUR HEART. Water those seeds with the words I have spoken over you, and watch them grow. Fix your eyes on me and not the natural circumstances, for you do not always know what is happening in the spiritual realm.

The winds of change are blowing. Embrace change, child; do not resist. Simply let go and let my wind carry you. While you are waiting on my winds of change, and the seeds I planted to sprout, focus on the simple blessings of each day. Be present with me in the moment. I am with you. Let my peace guide you.

Faithful and absolutely trustworthy is He who is calling you [to Himself for your salvation], and He will do it [He will fulfill His call by making you holy, guarding you, watching over you, and protecting you as His own.

– 1 THESSALONIANS 5:24

March 3

BE CAREFUL NOT TO THROW your pearls before swine. I love you. You are precious to me. I am lovingly and tenderly nurturing you. I will give you the food and water you need. You shall lack nothing when you are with me. I am the vine and you are the branches. Apart from me there is no LIFE. Being connected to me is the only hope for the production of good fruit.

Let me guide and direct your steps. I will always be with you. Do not rely on your own strength or skills, for they come from me and I can give you more. It is not about your ability, it is about mine. Remember that. I have come so that you may have LIFE. Rely on me. I am for you!

Therefore as you have received Christ Jesus the Lord, walk in [union with] Him [reflecting His character in the things you do and say—living lives that lead others away from sin], having been deeply rooted [in Him] and now being continually built up in Him and [becoming increasingly more] established in your faith, just as you were taught, and overflowing in it with gratitude.

– COLOSSIANS 2:6-7

March 4

I LOVE YOU. DO NOT EVER LOSE SIGHT OF THAT.
I will go before you and make a way. I have set your feet on solid ground, and I will continue to do so as you walk by my side. Do not wander into the deep without my hand to hold. Stay away from the dark waters. I am LIFE. I am the answer to the questions your heart cries. Look, see, and know that I am God, and I am love.

I am opening a door for you leading to a stage where a choir is performing. Be a part of that choir. The invitation is always open to you. The song is most beautiful when sung together. If one part is missing, it changes the entire voice. So it is with my body.

Do not let your feet get stuck in the quicksand of worry and fear. I will provide. I will prepare.

Love is to be sincere and active [the real thing—without guile and hypocrisy]. Hate what is evil [detest all ungodliness, do not tolerate wickedness]; hold on tightly to what is good.

– ROMANS 12:9

March 5

THE PLACE OF REST IS WHERE you will hear about all I have for you. Learn how to experience rest in any situation and you will hear me. I love you. Make sure you never stop hearing me say that. You are awesome. The path ahead is peaceful because I am there.

I am the light of the world. The darkness is great, but I am greater. I have come to bring LIFE. My voice is all around you. Be still and know that I am here, and that I go with you.

I have heard your prayers and I am dropping blessings on your house. Walk in the knowledge that my glory is here with you. I am at home here with you. Let this be a place of worship. I love you so much. Let your life proclaim who I am!

For He has rescued us and has drawn us to Himself from the dominion of darkness, and has transferred us to the kingdom of His beloved Son, in whom we have redemption [because of His sacrifice, resulting in] the forgiveness of our sins [and the cancellation of sin's penalty].

– COLOSSIANS 1:13-14

March 6

MY ANSWER TO YOU IS, "YES." And that yes is found in Jesus. Pursue the goodness and rightness of my heart and you shall walk in light. Separate yourself from evil and from distractions intending to take you off of the narrow road, for the path that leads to destruction is wide. If it were not so, there would not be so many gathered on it. Its fruit is poison and chokes out LIFE.

Let the redeemed of the Lord say so. Touch my vulnerability. Fix your eyes on my smiling face, and righteousness, along with justice, shall pursue you. Like coattails or the train of a wedding dress, goodness and blessings surely follow my beloved bride.

Find your peace and identity in me. I am your strength. It is I who live in you, and that is where victory comes from. I have got you.

Surely goodness and mercy and unfailing love shall follow me all the days of my life, and I shall dwell forever [throughout all my days] in the house and in the presence of the Lord.

– PSALM 23:6

March 7

MY WAYS ARE NOT YOUR WAYS; neither are my thoughts your thoughts. No, for they are much higher. My purposes and plans go far beyond what you see on the surface. I will give you glimpses of what they are, but you must choose to trust me when you do not fully understand.

Trust that my plans and intentions are good. Trust that my love can, and will, sustain you through any trials along the way. We will journey together hand in hand. All you need is enough faith to take one step. Will you join me?

For My thoughts are not your thoughts, nor are your ways My ways," declares the Lord. "For as the heavens are higher than the earth, so are My ways higher than your ways and My thoughts higher than your thoughts.

– ISAIAH 55:8-9

March 8

COME TO ME AND LIVE. No matter what is going on, I will always provide a place for you to lay your head. Do not worry about the things you need for life. I have already provided them. The things you want are also in my hands. I am alive and active, watching over my word to perform it.

If you find shelter underneath my wings, you will not be destroyed no matter how powerful the storm seems to be. It does not mean you will not be touched, but you shall remain solid.

Then the Lord said to me, "You have seen well, for I am [actively] watching over My word to fulfill it."

– JEREMIAH 1:12

O my God, in You I [have unwavering] trust [and I rely on You with steadfast confidence], do not let me be ashamed or my hope in You be disappointed; do not let my enemies triumph over me.

– PSALM 25:2

March 9

YOU ARE GROWING UP IN ME. You have matured in some areas and you continue to mature in more. I will take you deeper into who I am. Lean steadily on me and find your support. I will lead you. There is much to discover.

I love you so much. You are sweet wine on my lips. You are pleasing, delightful, and intoxicating. You honor me when you honor others. Everything you do is for me. So look to me for your reward and not to what the world can give you.

But without faith it is impossible to [walk with God and] please Him, for whoever comes [near] to God must [necessarily] believe that God exists and that He rewards those who [earnestly and diligently] seek Him.

— HEBREWS 11:6

March 10

TAKE A MOMENT AND LET THE DUST SETTLE, CHILD.
I have many things to show you in your current situation. But there are times you spin your wheels and kick up dust that blinds you. This causes much unrest and anxiety.

Grab hold of my peace; rest in my presence until you are able to see what I am trying to show you. Do not allow your adversary to pull you ahead. When the dust settles, you will have clear vision to see. Your mind will then be at peace to go forward in victory!

So, as God's own chosen people, who are holy [set apart, sanctified for His purpose] and well-beloved [by God Himself], put on a heart of compassion, kindness, humility, gentleness, and patience [which has the power to endure whatever injustice or unpleasantness comes, with good temper];

– COLOSSIANS 3:12

He who is slow to anger has great understanding [and profits from his self-control], but he who is quick-tempered exposes and exalts his foolishness [for all to see].

– PROVERBS 14:29

March 11

I LOVE YOU. DO NOT EVER CLOSE your ears to those words. You are the light in my eyes. I delight in you. Let that sink in and not just bounce off of your heart like a rubber ball. Let it impact you. Let it reach into the depths of your being.

Just look in the mirror and gaze at my dwelling place. You are intensely beautiful. Look past the lies your adversary loves to whisper and see the truth. You are a special piece of my gorgeous bride. You have a permanent place in my heart. There is a space in my heart that only you can fill.

Love is the greatest gift of all. Miracles are to bring people into my arms. Chase love, and the rest will fall into place. I love your heart.

In Him [and in fellowship with one another] you also are being built together into a dwelling place of God in the Spirit.

– EPHESIANS 2:22

And now there remain: faith [abiding trust in God and His promises], hope [confident expectation of eternal salvation], love [unselfish love for others growing out of God's love for me], these three [the choicest graces]; but the greatest of these is love.

– 1 CORINTHIANS 13:13

March 12

I WILL NEVER LET GO OF YOU. Even when you are not aware of me, I am holding you together. Do not squirm against my grasp. If you want me to let go, I will. I can be sent away. I can be directed to the corner to watch. But that will not be *my* choice. It is up to you to allow my will to be done in your life.

I love you more than you could know. My love is deeper than anything in the natural world around you. My love is supernatural.

And He Himself existed and is before all things, and in Him all things hold together. [His is the controlling, cohesive force of the universe.]

– COLOSSIANS 1:17

March 13

I CHERISH, ADORE, AND LOVE YOU. You are a delight to me. I have not forgotten about you, and I never will. I have amazing plans for you. Trust me and seek to understand me.

There is a fundamental misunderstanding on what is important. The world and its systems use one scale, and I use another. Mine is the only one that will count in the end.

I will continue to do the work I started in you. I am working to refine your core until all that is left is pure gold. Let the beauty of who you are radiate outwards from within. You are truly magnificent. I love you so much. You are truly valuable to me.

"And I will bring the third part through the fire, refine them as silver is refined, and test them as gold is tested. They will call on My name, and I will listen and answer them; I will say, 'They are My people,' and they will say, 'The Lord is my God.'".

– ZECHARIAH 13:9

March 14

WHAT DO YOU WANT? What is it that you want to pursue? Let's go after it together. Cut off the boulder that is weighing you down. Only a small string ties it on.

I will breathe strength into you. Learn to rest in me and I will refresh you. I will give you all that you need. Wait for me to bring you the things that you will need for the road ahead.

What I want is for you to be more like me. I have a plan for you. Do not worry for it is a good one. If I create a plan for you, I will also be the one to lead you through it. It is okay to trust me. Follow me and focus on today, on what is in front of you. I will prepare you for the things to come.

For we are His workmanship [His own master work, a work of art], created in Christ Jesus [reborn from above—spiritually transformed, renewed, ready to be used] for good works, which God prepared [for us] beforehand [taking paths which He set], so that we would walk in them [living the good life which He prearranged and made ready for us].

– EPHESIANS 2:10

March 15

PROMOTION IN ME IS FAR GREATER than promotion in the world. The world hands out temporary rewards, but I hand out everlasting LIFE and everlasting rewards. I have so many good gifts for my children, but many are standing with their arms crossed and refusing to take them from me. Their hearts yearn for them, but the blocks established in their minds keep them from seeing that I want them, that I love them, and that I really do have gifts for them.

I want you, I love you, and I really do have many gifts for you. It is okay to receive.

If you then, evil (sinful by nature) as you are, know how to give good and advantageous gifts to your children, how much more will your Father who is in heaven [perfect as He is] give what is good and advantageous to those who keep on asking Him.

– MATTHEW 7:11

March 16

IN MY PRESENCE IS FULLNESS OF JOY! In my presence is peace, rest, and answers to your questions. Bring me your frustrations and problems, for wisdom and understanding come from me. Invite me into your day and together we will navigate through any trials that come. When you involve me, you will be victorious.

Passionately pursue wisdom. Command the fog of confusion to be lifted, and it will go. Seek wisdom in every area of your life, for my wisdom is the fertilizer that brings forth LIFE.

Ideas, thoughts, visions, and dreams are like seeds sown into the ground. Growth will never take place without my wisdom, and any sprouts will quickly whither and die. Apply my wisdom to each situation and you will see LIFE spring forth in all areas!

You will show me the path of life; In Your presence is fullness of joy; In Your right hand there are pleasures forevermore.

– PSALM 16:11

For the Lord gives [skillful and godly] wisdom; from His mouth come knowledge and understanding.

– PROVERBS 2:6

March 17

I LOVE YOU. YOU ARE MINE, I am yours, and I will never let you go. I am asking you to never let me *go*. Watch out for obstacles that seek to distract you, and hinder you from moving forward.

I am so proud of you. Thanks for being courageous. If you are willing, I can make you a blessing to many.

I hear every single cry of your heart. You can trust me fully and completely. I will never hang you out to dry. When that happens, it is because you have moved out ahead of me and made choices I was not leading you to make. Stay in the shadow of my wings and you will remain protected and fully cared for. I love you so much. I will never take my hand away from you.

And I will make you a great nation, and I will bless you [abundantly], and make your name great (exalted, distinguished); and you shall be a blessing [a source of great good to others];

– GENESIS 12:2

March 18

I LOVE YOU SO MUCH. I will keep you steady on unsteady ground. Grab onto me and you will not fall through the cracks. Watch me, not the road. Learn to look for me all around you.

I am growing fruit in you for others to experience. People around you will comment on your character. They will feel love radiating from you. Love is the fruit, and it is ripe, sweet, and attracts many. Do not be afraid to give it away.

Sometimes you guard the fruit I have grown in you. You throw up a fence and keep it to yourself. Let others take from you what I have done in you. Give it freely, for who can resist the sweet fragrance it lets off. You have my LIFE within you. Give it to those who come.

But the fruit of the Spirit [the result of His presence within us] is love [unselfish concern for others], joy, [inner] peace, patience [not the ability to wait, but how we act while waiting], kindness, goodness, faithfulness, gentleness, self-control. Against such things there is no law.

– GALATIANS 5:22-23

March 19

LIVING IN JOY DOES NOT MEAN wearing rose colored glasses. If something is not good, you cannot make it good by lying to yourself. But it *does* mean that you look for the good rather than the bad. Let joy guide you instead of skepticism, bitterness, or anguish.

I am joy. To be filled with me is to be filled with joy. Come to the river and lay your burdens downs. Rest in my love for you.

Joy comes from my heart and pours into yours. When you are grafted into me, joy becomes a seed planted in your heart. Heaviness and despair will try to keep it from ever sprouting. Darkness and hopelessness will try to crush it. But they shall not prevail.

Joy is bright and brings LIFE to any circumstance. Joy is tied to identity. My joy comes from knowing who you are – My beloved child. That knowledge causes the seed to grow and take deep root.

Joy can be snuffed out, as can peace, kindness, and all the rest. You must choose to let it live in you.

And now my head will be lifted up above my enemies around me; in His tent I will offer sacrifices with shouts of joy; I will sing, yes, I will sing praises to the Lord.

– PSALM 27:6

March 20

I AM IN YOU. THAT MEANS JOY IS IN YOU. The journey is discovering what is keeping it from shining. What is stacked on top of the joy that is already in you?

There are varying degrees of blocks. For some, no joy gets through at all. For others, it is a like a single ray of sunshine through a window. But I want it to be a full on blast of light. The obstructions matter, and I do not want them to hinder you any longer. So let me uncover the obstructions.

O clap your hands, all you people; shout to God with the voice of triumph and songs of joy. For the Lord Most High is to be feared [and worshiped with awe-inspired reverence and obedience]; He is a great King over all the earth.

– PSALM 47:1-2

My lips will shout for joy when I sing praises to You, and my soul, which You have redeemed.

– PSALM 71:23

March 21

YOU ARE MIGHTY AND I LOVE YOU SO MUCH. I am proud of you in all the ways you honor others and me. I am with you, and I will never leave you on your own.

I am LIFE; LIFE is produced through everyone who calls on my name. Take a bite of my fruit. Let it fill you with its sweet flesh and aroma. Let love be your guide. Love will usher in compassion.

I do not ever want relationships to be severed. The ministry I came to bring is one of reconciliation. As much as it depends on you, live in peace with everyone.

I will pour myself out on you and make the lilies of your heart grow. Find your rest in me. I have overcome the things that bind you. I am your sword and shield. I will fight for you. I am unlocking myself for you and am opening the door to the deeper things of my heart. There is so much love there, more than you can understand. It is a deep and endless ocean for you.

Never repay anyone evil for evil. Take thought for what is right and gracious and proper in the sight of everyone. If possible, as far as it depends on you, live at peace with everyone.

– ROMANS 12:17-18

March 22

CONSIDER A PIT OF MUD with many people content to wallow in it. A man comes with a hose and begins washing the people, cleaning off all of the mud. They become very uncomfortable because they are used to, and love, the mud. Once they are clean, they run right back to the mud and call others to join them.

There is a beautiful house next to the pit where they can be clean and live in splendor, but they refuse. They see the house as the mud pit, and the mud pit as the house. If they would only clean their dirty eyes, they would be free.

I am the man with the hose, and the house is mine. You can live with me instead of living in the mud. But if you love the mud, you will not see the beauty that exists in front of you.

O Jerusalem, Jerusalem, who murders the prophets and stones [to death] those [messengers] who are sent to her [by God]! How often I wanted to gather your children together [around Me], as a hen gathers her chicks under her wings, and you were unwilling.

– MATTHEW 23:37

March 23

DECREE LIFE AND ABUNDANCE from the throne room because you are here with me in the heavenly places. I have assigned you a seat right next to me. Be encouraged and remain steadfast. I have so many great things for you. Speak my words and watch them become a reality in your life. I will open your heart to see even more of my kingdom.

As the grass hardly seems to grow when it is being watched, there are times it seems like I am not moving at all. But I tell you the truth; I am moving and working for you. I am completing the work that I started in you. I am drawing you ever closer to my heart. You will see me even more clearly than you do now. I *want* to reveal myself to you. Let my peace inhabit you and your home. Pursue the things that give LIFE, the things that shine brightly from within.

I am blowing through you like a fresh wind. Rejoice, for I have overcome. I will inspire the stories of your heart. You make me smile.

Rejoice in the Lord always [delight, take pleasure in Him]; again I will say, rejoice! Let your gentle spirit [your graciousness, unselfishness, mercy, tolerance, and patience] be known to all people. The Lord is near.

– PHILIPPIANS 4:4-5

March 24

I TAKE DELIGHT IN YOU, my precious child. I know you fully and I love you, your quirks and all! I especially love the little things that set you apart from others. I have created you to be unique, for you have a calling on your life specific to your gifts and personality.

Walk confidently in your uniqueness. Do not despise my masterpiece, for I took great care in weaving the tapestry of your being. You have not been created to blend in. I am calling you to stand out and sparkle. It grieves me when you compare yourself with others, your gifts and calling with their gifts and calling. Be you, and be you to the fullest.

For You formed my innermost parts; You knit me [together] in my mother's womb. I will give thanks and praise to You, for I am fearfully and wonderfully made; wonderful are Your works, and my soul knows it very well.

– PSALM 139:13-14

I LOVE YOU. Continue to look to me as I lead you into new territory, for I am doing a new thing in your life. Lean not on your own understanding, but seek me for wisdom. Look to me for your strength. Do not let fear keep you from walking this journey. Speak my words and anoint people with my love.

I long for you and my heart goes out for you. You are dearly loved. Be still and know that I am God. I am pouring my spirit out on my people. Through my love, you will minister in power! Signs and wonders follow those who believe. Signs and wonders will follow you. My children will be exalted. Do not be afraid, for I am with you every step.

These signs will accompany those who have believed: in My name they will cast out demons, they will speak in new tongues; 18 they will pick up serpents, and if they drink anything deadly, it will not hurt them; they will lay hands on the sick, and they will get well."

– MARK 16:17-18

March 26

I AM YOUR FLASHLIGHT, and I will light the way for you. I am the Lord. I am the first and last.

I love you. You are precious to me, and I do not want you to ever forget it. I will always let you know just how much you mean to me. Wait on me and do not be afraid. I am the pillar of fire that moves before you. Do not run ahead of me or you will not be able to see, and the danger will increase. Be still and remember who I am. I am for you. I am on your side. Seek me and my heart will be revealed. It will open up to you like a flower.

Do not allow anything to come and remove you from your place of rest beside me.

The [presence of the] Lord was going before them by day in a pillar (column) of cloud to lead them along the way, and in a pillar of fire by night to give them light, so that they could travel by day and by night. He did not withdraw the pillar of cloud by day, nor the pillar of fire by night, from going before the people.
    – EXODUS 13:21-22

March 27

YOU ARE MY PLANTING, AND FROM YOU I will grow much fruit. Be still and know that I am leading you faithfully. Take steps as I gently nudge you along. There are enemies who seek your destruction, but stay behind me and I will protect you. I will guard you from the arrows that are being fired with intent to steal, kill, and destroy.

I will give you LIFE where there has been death, strength where there has been weakness, and beauty where there have been ashes. I am the one who raises up dry bones, and I will resurrect hope in the hopeless. I am the Father of Lights and you are a child of the light. You are a child of the day. I have anointed you with my oil and sent you out to anoint others.

I have set my crown on your head. It shines with love, and that is how others will know you are mine. They will see my love radiating from you with the intensity of my kingdom.

Every good thing given and every perfect gift is from above; it comes down from the Father of lights [the Creator and Sustainer of the heavens], in whom there is no variation [no rising or setting] or shadow cast by His turning [for He is perfect and never changes].

– JAMES 1:17

March 28

I AM REVEALING THE PATH BEFORE YOU. Lean on my shoulders and go at my pace. Relax and continue to find rest in me. Seek me for everything you need.

I am increasing my presence in your midst, and I will lead you into prosperity. I will not let your foot strike against the sharp rock. Watch out for the snares of the enemy. Stay alert and on guard. I am going before you and I am watching behind. Stay close to me so you can hear my specific directions. Welcome wise counsel into your life. Do not reject those I have sent to help you.

Your cries have reached my ears, and I am moving in ways you cannot see at this time. But take heart and have confidence in my ability to deliver you. I love you. Though I want you to experience my love, there are times in which you must simply *rely* on it. Trust that I see so much more than you and that I already have the answer.

We have come to know [by personal observation and experience], and have believed [with deep, consistent faith] the love which God has for us. God is love, and the one who abides in love abides in God, and God abides continually in him.

– 1 JOHN 4:16

March 29

WALK WITH ME, CHILD. There are times we will walk together through dry, hot, desert places, and there are times we will walk through lush green forests. We will walk through fragrant and beautiful gardens, the lowest valleys, and the highest mountaintops. There is only one thing that remains constant: My presence.

When we are in difficult places, know that I am still here and that I am holding you. I am here to comfort and carry you when you cannot take another step on your own. I will give you my strength and encourage you to press on.

When we walk through the beautiful places, I am there as well. I am here to rejoice with you, to skip and dance with you. I love your joy. I am, and will always be, your ever-present Daddy.

'Do not fear [anything], for I am with you; Do not be afraid, for I am your God. I will strengthen you, be assured I will help you; I will certainly take hold of you with My righteous right hand [a hand of justice, of power, of victory, of salvation].'
– ISAIAH 41:10

March 30

DO YOU BELIEVE THAT YOU ARE worth an abundance of blessings? Do you believe that I look at you with unfathomable love and desire to pour out so much more in your life? If an earthly father looks at his children and blesses them, then how much more do I, the perfect Father with perfect love, want to bless my children?

You have not because you ask not. You ask not because you have believed you are not worthy of it.

Now it is an extraordinary thing for one to willingly give his life even for an upright man, though perhaps for a good man [one who is noble and selfless and worthy] someone might even dare to die. But God clearly shows and proves His own love for us, by the fact that while we were still sinners, Christ died for us.

– ROMANS 5:7-8

March 31

I AM WITH YOU. Even in the places where there seems to be no light, your heart is shining brightly. Will clouds and fog extinguish my light? No! The light will continually beat against them and they will be destroyed.

Do not get your eyes fixed on the natural. There are things happening in the spiritual realm that you cannot always see in the natural. Hope is lost when you keep your eyes fixed on the natural. Even an elated heart fixed only on the natural is a sick heart. Guard your heart!

Come and rest, for I have made you a bed called PEACE; the covers are called FAITH.

For God, who said, "Let light shine out of darkness," is the One who has shone in our hearts to give us the Light of the knowledge of the glory and majesty of God [clearly revealed] in the face of Christ.

– 2 CORINTHIANS 4:6

April

Sing aloud to God our strength; shout for joy to the God of Jacob (Israel). "I am the Lord your God, who brought you up from the land of Egypt. Open your mouth wide and I will fill it."

– PSALM 81:1, 10

April 1

RESTORATION! I AM THE GOD OF RESTORATION and redemption. My eyes are searching your heart and my voice is calling out the joy I have deposited there. The joy will take root and grow into something that brings smiles like a large bubble does to a child.

Dance and rejoice with me. Lose yourself in the beauty of my presence. Let your heart be filled. I am here and I am ready to hold you. I am your strength. Take joy in what you are hearing, for I am destroying sorrow and pouring onto you the oil of gladness.

I am giving you beauty for ashes and a garment of praise for the spirit of heaviness. Look to me and find your peace. Let your heart be flooded with my love. Know today that I am for you. Smile at me with the knowledge that I am smiling back at you.

Sing aloud to God our strength; shout for joy to the God of Jacob (Israel). "I am the Lord your God, who brought you up from the land of Egypt. Open your mouth wide and I will fill it."

– PSALM 81:1, 10

April 2

I WILL REFRESH YOU WITH WATER. Smile as it covers your face. Dance in the joy that it brings. I love you, I am with you, and I am listening to you. Just listen to me. Return to the place of rest I have created for you. Do not fear failure, for I will be with you regardless of what happens. Just wait and I will show you the way.

Sometimes you struggle as to which way to go, or which path to take. But know that your choice has nothing to do with your worth and value. It has no bearing or weight on who I have created you to be.

I love you. It is not always about right or wrong, but rather what is better. It is about which road will allow me to accomplish more for you than the other. Will you trust where I am leading you?

When I am afraid, I will put my trust and faith in you. In God, whose word I praise; In God I have put my trust; I shall not fear. What can mere man do to me?

– PSALM 56:3-4

April 3

YOU HAVE STARTED TO SEE THE WAY your life might look in the years to come. When that happens, the future becomes a little more firmly planted in your mind. There is comfort in knowing, and in being able to see, how things might play out.

I would love to walk that road with you, and I will pour out my blessings. But what about the other roads that you cannot see? They are mysteries and seem unstable to you. But I am steadfast, and I am a sure foundation. You cannot see what those roads look like right now, but I can.

I have sent you a dove with an olive branch in its mouth. Keep peace at the center of your heart. There is no need for anxiety or fear. I will never leave you or abandon you; I love you way too much for that. No matter what path you choose, I will be doing whatever I can to keep you safe. No matter what, my abundance will always be available.

Trust in and rely confidently on the Lord with all your heart and do not rely on your own insight or understanding. In all your ways know and acknowledge and recognize Him, and He will make your paths straight and smooth [removing obstacles that block your way].

– PROVERBS 3:5-6

April 4

WHEN YOU RUN, RUN TO ME. I will always be here to hold you. You will never be alone.

I am holding the keys that unlock the options spread before you, and I will unlock the doors I want you to walk through. Do not try to force your way in. I will open the door that leads to the better way.

I have laid solid rock under your feet. Trust that it will always be there; I will never remove it. I am your eternal rock. I am your fortress and strong tower. Do not attach yourself to anyone's agenda. Instead, attach yourself to me.

Rightly divide what you hear; test it against my character, against my word.

Trust [confidently] in the Lord forever [He is your fortress, your shield, your banner], For the Lord God is an everlasting Rock [the Rock of Ages].

– ISAIAH 26:4

April 5

I HOLD THE KEYS TO MY HEART, and I am unlocking it for you. I am calling you inside to dwell in the deeper places of me. I want you to experience all I have to offer. I want you to share in my LIFE completely. This is all foundational. You need to walk before you run. Learn how to rest before you try to accelerate. Everything comes from the secret place with me.

I am standing on the water, asking you to leave the beach and come to me. I am your firm foundation! I will not be moved. I will not be overcome.

God is our refuge and strength [mighty and impenetrable], a very present and well-proved help in trouble. Therefore we will not fear, though the earth should change and though the mountains be shaken and slip into the heart of the seas, though its waters roar and foam, though the mountains tremble at its roaring. Selah.

There is a river whose streams make glad the city of God, the holy dwelling places of the Most High. God is in the midst of her [His city], she will not be moved; God will help her when the morning dawns.

– PSALM 46:1-5

April 6

I LOVE YOU, AND I AM HERE WITH YOU. You are so beautiful. I cannot wait for you to see me in all my glory, and to experience the change that will happen on that day. My love is so much more than you can imagine. The power of it is completely transforming, even to those already in the secret place of my heart. The depth you will experience in the days ahead is matchless. My love is simply the most powerful thing in existence.

Enter my sweet embrace. I am in you and you are in me. I have opened your ears to the sound of my voice. Recognize it and pay attention.

The wells of your heart run deep in me. I am the water you draw. I am the system that brings LIFE to the members of your body and the members of *my* body. Fix your eyes on me, and do not let your heart be troubled.

Peace I leave with you; My [perfect] peace I give to you; not as the world gives do I give to you. Do not let your heart be troubled, nor let it be afraid. [Let My perfect peace calm you in every circumstance and give you courage and strength for every challenge.]

– JOHN 14:27

April 7

I LOVE YOU, AND I AM SO PROUD OF YOU. You make me smile. Let me shower you with many gifts today. You are so special, and you make my heart sing. You are a sweet fragrance and a song factory. The songs that come out of you make me smile. Pursue my heart, and the music floating around you will always draw people into my love.

You are my beloved. Drink from me and be fulfilled: be renewed. If your anchor is in me, you will not fall. I am your firm foundation. Do not step off to the right or to the left, for there are cracks that split those paths: the paths of distraction.

Therefore become imitators of God [copy Him and follow His example], as well-beloved children [imitate their father]; and walk continually in love [that is, value one another—practice empathy and compassion, unselfishly seeking the best for others], just as Christ also loved you and gave Himself up for us, an offering and sacrifice to God [slain for you, so that it became] a sweet fragrance.

– EPHESIANS 5:1-2

April 8

I AM YOUR LIGHT, AND I WILL ILLUMINATE the way for you. Stick right beside me, and do not wander to the left or to the right, for that is where the robbers and murderers are. I am your shield, your fortress, and high tower.

There is no one like me. I am the breath of LIFE. What is impossible with man is possible with me. All things are possible through me. Do not be discouraged or dismayed at the dark hearts around you, for I can break through the thickest of nights. Do not allow your perceptions to dictate my ability.

I will give you LIFE. Cling to me, for I will never push you away. Rest in me, and let me exalt you. I will exalt you, but let me decide what that is going to look like.

My kingdom is established through Jesus, but those who labor in the field build it. The work can be hard, but the reward is worth the sweat. I have given you the tools to be successful in the field. Will you use them?

Ah Lord God! Behold, You have made the heavens and the earth by Your great power and by Your outstretched arm! There is nothing too difficult or too wonderful for You—

– JEREMIAH 32:17

April 9

I AM CALLING YOU OUT, MY PRECIOUS CHILD. I am calling you to take steps of faith. It is time to get outside of your comfort zone. Do not be afraid of getting it wrong, for I see your heart of trust and obedience.

Picture an unlit pathway of pavers. The paver will illuminate as you take a step, but only as your foot makes the connection. A way has been planned, but sometimes the ultimate destination is unknown. See this as an adventure and not a terrifying trek, for I am with you.

As I walk with you, there will be times that I go ahead like a shield. Other times I will stay at your side, and simply hold your hand.

It is the Lord who goes before you; He will be with you. He will not fail you or abandon you. Do not fear or be dismayed.

– DEUTERONOMY 31:8

April 10

I LOVE YOU! I AM LEADING YOU; do not be afraid of the unknown. I will give you directions if you ask. I am the Lord your God and I lead with love. If you have ears to hear, you will hear. Do not conform to the patterns of the world. Do not compromise the truth I have hidden in your heart.

I love you; you are so special to me. I want to hold you, laugh with you, and cry with you. I want to be your LIFE. Let everything that you do bring honor and glory to my name. Let not the work of your hands be separated from my love.

There are times when you judge the fruit of your life as insignificant and small, but I say it is full and beautiful; it is full of sweet flavor.

And do not be conformed to this world [any longer with its superficial values and customs], but be transformed and progressively changed [as you mature spiritually] by the renewing of your mind [focusing on godly values and ethical attitudes], so that you may prove [for yourselves] what the will of God is, that which is good and acceptable and perfect [in His plan and purpose for you].

– ROMANS 12:2

CONSIDER TWO WELLS. One holds water that will refresh and quench your thirst while the other holds stale water that will only increase your thirst. They look the same to you, and you are unable to decide which is which. But I know the answer. Ask me and I will tell you which well will bring you LIFE.

Discernment is the key because many things can look identical. Discernment is something to be practiced and developed. Do not venture out on your own. Stay close to me and I will show you the things that of me and the things that are not. Spend time with me so you know my voice. I want you to be able to hear me when I speak to you.

I want to lead you through life. I have so many beautiful plans for you. Stay close and let me lead you step by step.

But solid food is for the [spiritually] mature, whose senses are trained by practice to distinguish between what is morally good and what is evil.

– HEBREWS 5:14

Teach me good judgment (discernment) and knowledge, for I have believed and trusted and relied on Your commandments.

– PSALM 119:66

April 12

I AM LIFTING THE VEIL that covers your face. I want to get to know you more and more, but there are times when you appear unwilling. I desire to make my home in your heart and love you from the inside out.

Let all of your fears fall to the ground and they will be trampled by my perfect love for you. Because I am in you, you are an overcomer. My strength delivers the captives. I am the redeemer; I am *your* redeemer. I will lead you as you stay by my side.

You must open your heart before there can be intimacy between us. Find my arms. I am right here. Let me hold and comfort you. I am safe, and I love you so much. My thoughts are for you, and I am the warm blanket that covers you.

Behold, I stand at the door [of the church] and continually knock. If anyone hears My voice and opens the door, I will come in and eat with him (restore him), and he with Me

– REVELATION 3:20

April 13

CONSIDER A NEEDLE PULLING THREAD. I am the ultimate creator. I fashion clothes and garments for my children that they never thought they would be able to wear. Having beautiful righteous garments is not out of your reach. I have designed a set just for you, but you must claim it.

Come to me so that your joy may be complete. It is not mind over matter, but rather letting the truth become reality. It is opening up to the truth and letting it blow through you like a breeze. Just let it happen. Do not strive. Just fall into me.

I will rejoice greatly in the Lord, my soul will exult in my God; for He has clothed me with garments of salvation, He has covered me with a robe of righteousness, as a bridegroom puts on a turban, and as a bride adorns herself with her jewels.

– ISAIAH 61:10

April 14

I LOVE YOU SO MUCH; you are so special to me. You are the most beautiful of all creation. I see my reflection in you. All of creation was built for you to enjoy, for us to enjoy together.

I know the plans and purposes to which I have called you. Everything I prepare for you has great meaning. You want to change the world? So do I, so let's do it together.

The path I have laid out for you is special and unique. Do not compare yourself to others. You will never be irrelevant. You will never be insignificant. The voice that tells you different is a liar. You are forever on the forefront of my heart. I have a billboard in heaven with your face on it. Follow me, and let your light shine before the world.

We do not have the audacity to put ourselves in the same class or compare ourselves with some who [supply testimonials to] commend themselves. When they measure themselves by themselves and compare themselves with themselves, they lack wisdom and behave like fools.

– 2 CORINTHIANS 10:12

April 15

I ADORE YOU. You are so special and significant. I am here. I am the wine for your wineskin, and I will expand you. You will overflow with my love and desire. Not because of what you have done, or will do, but because of who you are and how I have made you. You carry the light of the world; you carry me.

Stand firm and do not be afraid, for I am with you. Though chaos may swarm, I have already delivered you. Wait on me to clear the way. Do not move until I nudge you forward. It will be safe, but only if you stay with me. I am your protector; I am your provider.

Do not be afraid. Learn how to pray, and press into me. There will be change, and there will be resurrection. I am your bread, and I am your drink. Consume me and you will become like me.

So Abraham named that place The Lord Will Provide. And it is said to this day, "On the mountain of the Lord it will be seen and provided.

– GENESIS 22:14

The young lions lack [food] and grow hungry, but they who seek the Lord will not lack any good thing.

– PSALM 34:10

April 16

SOMETIMES THE CROWN OF GLORY I place on the heads of my kids is viewed as a crown of suffering. But, lift up your eyes as I touch your head. I am not the source of pain and suffering, but the answer for it. I am your redeemer and your restoration. I am the healing balm on your head. I am your anchor, an ever-present help in time of need.

There is no need for you to be on your knees when I have called you into my arms. There is no need for tears of despair when I am the joy in you. Take off that cloak of heaviness and stand under the power of my love. I am showing you the way to my heart.

I love you and I am here for you. Do not hide your eyes, but fix them on me. The enemy is not strong enough to keep me from doing what I have come to do in your life.

And He will wipe away every tear from their eyes; and there will no longer be death; there will no longer be sorrow and anguish, or crying, or pain; for the former order of things has passed away.

– REVELATION 21:4

April 17

CONSIDER A MOUSE IN A MAZE working as hard as it can to get to the cheese on the other side. It hits dead end after dead end, but finally makes its way to the cheese. It never gives up.

My heart is calling to you and I am inviting you to find it. There may be some missteps and wrong turns along the way, but I will never remove my heart from you.

I will always be there, but it will take perseverance to gain all my heart has for you. And it is so much greater than you can imagine. If you get stuck, call to me and I will help you find the way. I will light your path. Speak to the obstacles and watch them move out of the way. I want you to find all that I have for you.

Ask and keep on asking and it will be given to you; seek and keep on seeking and you will find; knock and keep on knocking and the door will be opened to you

– MATTHEW 7:7

April 18

MY CARES AND PRIORITIES are not always different from yours. You can trust that I care about, and value, the same things you do. This is essential to being able to release the desires of your heart to me and truly rest.

I am a soft wind across the ocean of your heart. I have overcome the storms and heavy winds that come to churn the waters. Remain in me and you will remain in peace. I have overcome the world. I am the great gardener of your being. Let the petals of your heart reach out, and up, to me. I alone can provide the nourishment you need. I prune as necessary to produce a plant that is useful for every good work.

Even though there can be hard times, do not ever question my love for you. It is much higher than the tallest mountain.

In peace [and with a tranquil heart] I will both lie down and sleep, For You alone, O Lord, make me dwell in safety and confident trust.

– PSALM 4:8

April 19

I HAVE GIVEN YOU GREAT POWER and authority. Your words carry the weight of heaven. Speak peace into the storms of life. When things surround you and threaten to spin out of control, speak peace into the storm and it will settle down. The enemy will do whatever he can to keep your mouth closed. Trust that I will be there, and open your mouth so my words can flow forth.

Lead by serving. Look for ways to exalt and honor others. Many of the true leaders in my kingdom are little known and little recognized. The first will be last and the last will be first.

I am opening my heart to you. Follow me into LIFE.

So those who are last [in this world] shall be first [in the world to come], and those who are first, last.

– MATTHEW 20:16

April 20

DO NOT EVER BELIEVE THE LIE that I do not want to speak to you. That is the voice of the enemy whispering in your ear. I desire relationship with you. I will never keep my voice far from you. Allow me to build a stronghold of this truth in your heart.

Pick up your sword and shield and make yourself ready. The trail before you is overgrown. We will clear the path. Do not be dismayed at how things look on the outside, for I will cause you to see what is happening on the inside. I am pouring favor into your life. Step through the doors that it opens.

But the Lord said to Samuel, "Do not look at his appearance or at the height of his stature, because I have rejected him. For the Lord sees not as man sees; for man looks at the outward appearance, but the Lord looks at the heart."

– 1 SAMUEL 16:7

April 21

I LOVE YOU. ALL YOU NEED TO DO IS ASK, and I will show you things. Do not be afraid of what I have to reveal. I am tracing your footsteps all over the map for I have called you to explore the deeper things of my heart.

I understand that you cannot do everything. The tree has many branches. Each branch has its purpose. Blaze the trail you are on and let others blaze the trail they are on. That is what it means to work together.

You have a physical capacity for the work that needs to be done. You can only take so much, so I spread the assignments around. I have many workers, and each has their instructions. Do not enter into a job I have not assigned to you.

For just as in one [physical] body we have many parts, and these parts do not all have the same function or special use, so we, who are many, are [nevertheless just] one body in Christ, and individually [we are] parts one of another [mutually dependent on each other].

– ROMANS 12:4-5

April 22

YOU ARE SO SPECIAL TO ME. You are like honey on my lips. Your breath is sweet like rain.

I enjoy speaking to others *through* you. They are drawn to me by the way you live and the words you speak.

I want you to know that I am here. Even in the midst of fog so thick you cannot see, I am here. I will guide your footsteps and lead you on. Do not be afraid. Though you may not see the road, it is *my* road you are on and I know everything about it.

Trust me because I love you. The enemy shows you flashes of images meant to cause fear, but I have overcome. Listen to my voice and take another step. The sun is shining!

Even though I walk through the [sunless] valley of the shadow of death, I fear no evil, for You are with me; your rod [to protect] and Your staff [to guide], they comfort and console me. You prepare a table before me in the presence of my enemies. You have anointed and refreshed my head with oil; my cup overflows.

– PSALM 23:4-5

April 23

BLESSED ARE THOSE WHO FOLLOW ME, for their light will never be extinguished. I am growing and maturing the gifts I have given you. I love you and have plans for you. You are my beloved child. Trust in me. I will give you the desires of your heart.

There is not one thing you care about that does not make an impact on my heart. Rest in me. I love you and I am holding you. You are my delight. Let the waters of my love rise around you. My love is an ocean; set your sail.

Do not strive to do, but rest and be. You must be still in order to receive.

You visit the earth and make it overflow [with water]; you greatly enrich it; the stream of God is full of water; you provide their grain, when You have prepared the earth.

– PSALM 65:9

April 24

WHEREVER YOU CARRY MY LIGHT, darkness flees. I do not abide in the darkness, but I will invade and overthrow it. I am a warrior of light exposing any deception clouding the eyes of my children. Like the grains of sand on the shore, so are the lies my children have believed. This is why I came – to destroy the works of the devil; I will destroy them in your life.

I am the truth! If you keep your eyes on me, you will never be blinded by the dark schemes of your adversary. I will faithfully lead you around every winding corner the path has to offer. There is no need to fear, for I have gone before you. I am also standing guard behind.

And you will know the truth [regarding salvation], and the truth will set you free [from the penalty of sin]."
                                                    – JOHN 8:32

The one who practices sin [separating himself from God, and offending Him by acts of disobedience, indifference, or rebellion] is of the devil [and takes his inner character and moral values from him, not God]; for the devil has sinned and violated God's law from the beginning. The Son of God appeared for this purpose, to destroy the works of the devil.

                                                    – 1 JOHN 3:8

YOU MUST RECEIVE MY LOVE WELL in order to love well. My love is deep; it gives meaning and ascribes purpose, worth, and significance.

If you let me, I will handle the floodgates in your life. Listen to me as you commit to different opportunities. I will help you decide if you should, or should not, walk through the door. Do not be afraid to say no. I understand your body and what it can handle. I will not lead you into something that will destroy you physically. Not every opportunity is something you should step into. Detach yourself from the need to meet every single request. Boundaries are a testimony of my character unfolding in you.

Yes, You are my rock and my fortress; for Your name's sake You will lead me and guide me.

– PSALM 31:3

April 26

BE GRACIOUS AND FULL OF LOVE. I am so proud of you. I will give you more influence as I see that what I have already given you is accomplishing my will in your life and in the lives of those around you. I love it when you show love. You do it so well. I will show you how to love in even greater ways.

Love is your foundation; it is how you reset your heart. It is your nature and your character. Love never fails. It seeks to build and never tear down. Love stands in the light when those around you want to fade into darkness. Love is a beacon. The world is looking for those who will actually stand against immorality by the way they live. Words are lost, but actions are remembered.

You will stand for love and your actions will be remembered. I will give you the tools you need to shine brightly before the world.

Now no one lights a lamp and then covers it with a container [to hide it], or puts it under a bed; instead, he puts it on a lampstand, so that those who come in may see the light.

– LUKE 8:16

April 27

I AM A MIGHTY WAVE TO SOME, a stream of water to others, and a small trickle to a few. But many are still completely dry. Pull on the chains and release the flow into the valleys and deserts. My children will come to drink. Invite them to get their fill and wander into the deeper portions of my heart. There have been times in which you have done this without even realizing it.

See, my burden is easy and my yoke is light. Come to me if you feel heavy and weighed down and I will give you rest. Joy and peace run together in the heart that is anchored to me. Love, hope, peace, and joy are anchored in my love.

He turned the desert into pools of water and the parched ground into flowing springs; there he brought the hungry to live, and they founded a city where they could settle.

– PSALM 107:35-36

April 28

I HAVE CALLED YOU FORTH from the shadows and instructed you in the ways of LIFE. Now shine brightly! Take the light of my LIFE to those in darkness.

Do not grow weary of well doing. When you feel your strength draining, lift your eyes to me and I will refill you. That is a promise. Do not let the clouds of frustration cover your heart. An unloving attitude is not from me. It never is. Remember that, and fight the lies telling you that the end justifies the means. It is my kindness that draws my children to repentance.

You, therefore, have no excuse, you who pass judgment on someone else, for at whatever point you judge another, you are condemning yourself, because you who pass judgment do the same things. Now we know that God's judgment against those who do such things is based on truth. So when you, a mere human being, pass judgment on them and yet do the same things, do you think you will escape God's judgment? Or do you show contempt for the riches of his kindness, forbearance and patience, not realizing that God's kindness is intended to lead you to repentance?

– ROMANS 2:1-4

April 29

THE MORE YOU PURSUE MY HEART, the more you will naturally live in the abundant LIFE I came to bring. It is supposed to be that way. The life I lived should be the natural way to live. Let it become natural for you. The things I lead you to do and say to others will not be as unusual as they used to be. That is what happens when you are transformed into my image.

I love it when you let me know that I am special to you. I cannot help but smile when I look at you. I have come so that your joy might be full!

Do not let fear keep you from hearing some things that I would love for you to hear. You are royalty sitting on a throne of love. You know what a throne looks like, but what does love look like? Take away the chair and find your knees. It is the position of a servant. There is no greater joy than that birthed from self-sacrificial love.

Whoever says he lives in Christ [that is, whoever says he has accepted Him as God and Savior] ought [as a moral obligation] to walk and conduct himself just as He walked and conducted Himself.

– 1 JOHN 2:6

April 30

LIKE A COOL WIND BLOWING IN THE NIGHT, so is my word against your heart. It is an ointment to the burns and traumas of the past. It is peace to the distressed. My joy is full and I give it freely. Take joy from me. It will sustain and preserve you.

Rest. Let me drop a blanket of rest over your shoulders. My arms are warmer than wool. My chest is a pillow softer than feathers. You are so special to me. I desire you and I love you. I really enjoy you; do not forget it. Live in that revelation, that truth.

I have clothed you in purple. White garments show your purity and purple your royalty. Wear them both.

The nations will see your righteousness and vindication [by God], and all kings [will see] your glory; and you will be called by a new name which the mouth of the Lord will designate. You will also be [considered] a crown of glory and splendor in the hand of the Lord, and a royal diadem [exceedingly beautiful] in the hand of your God.

– ISAIAH 62:2-3

This page intentionally left blank

May

Therefore we do not become discouraged [spiritless, disappointed, or afraid]. Though our outer self is [progressively] wasting away, yet our inner self is being [progressively] renewed day by day. For our momentary, light distress [this passing trouble] is producing for us an eternal weight of glory [a fullness] beyond all measure [surpassing all comparisons, a transcendent splendor and an endless blessedness]!

– 2 CORINTHIANS 4:16-17

I LOVE YOU AND I WILL SHOWER you with mercy. You are so special. You are my child and I long to hold you in my arms. I long to hold you in a tight embrace.

Do not be discouraged and do not lose heart. I am with you. Consult me and you will receive direction. Stick close by my side and you will see the way. Keep on letting me teach you truth. Do not be afraid. Practice discernment and it will continue to mature.

I am the God of wholeness, redemption, and restoration. I am not on the cross anymore. I am alive and reigning. I hold the keys to the storehouse of abundant LIFE!

Therefore we do not become discouraged [spiritless, disappointed, or afraid]. Though our outer self is [progressively] wasting away, yet our inner self is being [progressively] renewed day by day. For our momentary, light distress [this passing trouble] is producing for us an eternal weight of glory [a fullness] beyond all measure [surpassing all comparisons, a transcendent splendor and an endless blessedness]!

– 2 CORINTHIANS 4:16-17

May 2

HOW LONG, CHILD? How long will you continue to believe the lies about your identity? When will you receive and believe my truth? You are my beloved child. You are the one I pursue.

Do you see the rainbow I have placed in the sky? Do you see the beautiful flowers at your feet? Do you smell the sweet fragrance after the rain? All of these things are for you. I want you to know that I love and cherish you; my heart is for you and not against you.

It is so important to me that you know and walk in your true identity. Your time of walking in shame has come to an end. Your time of listening to lies has come to an end. Look at the glorious shoes I have placed before you. Have a seat, put them on, and walk confidently, knowing that I am in you and all around you. When you do not feel courageous, let my courage flow through you. I will be your strength, so walk tall.

But you are a chosen race, a royal priesthood, a consecrated nation, a [special] people for God's own possession, so that you may proclaim the excellencies [the wonderful deeds and virtues and perfections] of Him who called you out of darkness into His marvelous light.

– 1 PETER 2:9

YOU CAN ALWAYS RESET AND REST IN ME. In my presence is where you need to be, not just right now, but every moment throughout the day. I will hit that big, red reset button and get you firmly planted back on the right road.

Being in my presence gives your spirit the workout and recovery it needs. It is here with me that you are built up. Many of my children carry a spirit that is much larger than their physical appearance. In the same way, you can carry a presence much larger than your physical body. That will happen as you allow me to pour into you.

You know, we do not always have to talk. Sometimes we can just be together. I am comfortable with that. Are you? Come with me to the secret place and let me tell you wonderful things. Did you know I am still creating? Did you think my creative mind could be silenced?

For physical training is of some value, but godliness (spiritual training) is of value in everything and in every way, since it holds promise for the present life and for the life to come.

– 1 TIMOTHY 4:8

May 4

WHAT DO I WANT YOU TO BE? Who do I say you are? I love you; you are my child; you shine brightly. I see you, and I am with you. I will not ever leave you. I am holding your hand and leading you. Stay with me.

Pay close attention in the days that are ahead. I am placing glasses on your face so that you can see clearly. I am placing my aid in your ear so you can hear clearly. You will see and you will hear in a much greater way than you do now. It is my pleasure to do these things for you.

He said to them, "The mystery of the kingdom of God has been given to you [who have teachable hearts], but those who are outside [the unbelievers, the spiritually blind] get everything in parables, so that they will continually look but not see, and they will continually hear but not understand, otherwise they might turn [from their rejection of the truth] and be forgiven.

– MARK 4:11-12

CONSIDER A DEEP VALLEY surrounded and protected by high cliffs. In the valley is a brook with slow moving water and lush, green plants all around. Flowers of all different types and vibrant colors create a border. A light breeze rolls through, and the only sounds are the gentle movements of wildlife.

This is the secret place. I am here sitting beside the brook with a fishing pole. Come and sit next to me as I cast your burdens out into the water where they disappear. Let yourself be overcome by my peace.

Do not be afraid to be here with me. I love you. I am not here to point out what is wrong with you. I do not dwell on your failures; I shine a bright light on your successes.

He that dwelleth in the secret place of the most High shall abide under the shadow of the Almighty. I will say of the Lord, He is my refuge and my fortress: my God; in him will I trust.

– PSALM 91:1 (NIV)

May 6

I LOVE YOU. I WILL GO ahead of you and part the waters. I have claimed victory. It is a victory that no one can take away.

The sun can be bright and hot, but I am a cool breeze. I am refreshing and I am the balm for your cracked lips. I am life, hope, and peace. I am the passion within you. I am swirling and moving in your midst. Listen to my voice so that you can know what I am doing and where I want to lead you.

Can you hear me? Will you follow me?

The sheep that are My own hear My voice and listen to Me; I know them, and they follow Me. And I give them eternal life, and they will never, ever [by any means] perish; and no one will ever snatch them out of My hand.

– JOHN 10:27-28

May 7

CONSIDER TUMBLEWEED blowing through the desert with a person trapped inside. There are those who are blown around by the slightest change of wind. They are not steadfast and do not plant their feet. Because of this, everything is dry and cracked and they remain thirsty. There is no time for them to take root because they are blown somewhere else before they can become established.

Even when it feels like there is no solid ground to stand on, I can plant your feet. I can be the pool of cool water that will anchor your root system. My love and my heart are where your foundation is. My love is your solid foundation, and if you stand on it, you will stand strong. You will not be moved no matter how hard the wind blows.

So that we are no longer children [spiritually immature], tossed back and forth [like ships on a stormy sea] and carried about by every wind of [shifting] doctrine, by the cunning and trickery of [unscrupulous] men, by the deceitful scheming of people ready to do anything [for personal profit].

– EPHESIANS 4:14

I LOVE YOU. YOU ARE MINE. I hold you in my arms just like I have done so many times before. You are so precious to me. I will rock you when you cry and I will feed you when you are hungry. I am your source of LIFE.

I am the laughter in your heart and the freedom in your veins. I am the holiness your heart longs for and the intimacy you need. I am the great woodsman making a way for you in the forest.

The loudest wails of suffering, though heard and deeply cared about, are like whispers compared to the sound of my love and healing rushing in like many waters. The wound is loud, but my answer is louder.

Cast your burden on the Lord [release it] and He will sustain and uphold you; He will never allow the righteous to be shaken (slip, fall, fail).

– PSALM 55:22

I HAVE PLACED A GREAT CALLING on your life, and I am bringing you into it. The shoes you have on now are not the ones you will be wearing when you enter your calling in a more complete way. I am your flashlight so you can see in the dark. Seek me first and the kingdom will be opened to you.

Walk faithfully with me. Do not turn to the right or to the left, but keep your eyes on me. Look up to greater revelation and I will flood the eyes of your heart with it.

Fall into my arms. Do not hide your face from my open heart. Stay in my presence and believe that I want you there. Do not push me aside in an attempt for present glory. If you are faithful with a little, I will give you more.

His master said to him, 'Well done, good and faithful servant. You have been faithful and trustworthy over a little, I will put you in charge of many things; share in the joy of your master.

– MATTHEW 25:21

May 10

WALK WITH ME THROUGH THE GARDEN. Here are the sun and moon with fields of grass and animals. The earth is not evil though there is evil in it. I came to form, mold, and prepare you to establish my kingdom here. There is a day coming when all evil will be vanquished from the earth. I will make it like new.

There are many who only care about what the world has to offer. But others are gathered together reflecting my heart to the world's systems. They have the blood of the Lamb on their garments. I want you to join them. Are you ready?

Through God we will have victory, for He will trample down our enemies.

– PSALM 60:12

For our struggle is not against flesh and blood [contending only with physical opponents], but against the rulers, against the powers, against the world forces of this [present] darkness, against the spiritual forces of wickedness in the heavenly (supernatural) places.

– EPHESIANS 6:12

I LOVE YOU. REST IN ME. I am the living water and I will consume all of the fire that burns to destroy. You make me so happy. The gates are opening and you cannot imagine what lies on the other side. Stay close to the path I have marked out for you.

Your words are powerful. Just wait and see what I can accomplish through them. Let your life be a reflection of me and watch the broken get healed and restored. Just as I continue to knock down the walls erected between you and me, so will they fall in those around you as you speak the words I place in your heart. We will do this together. I am inviting you on this journey. Thank you for making yourself trustworthy. I will give you more since you have been faithful with little.

Open the gates, that the righteous nation may enter, the one that remains faithful and trustworthy.

– ISAIAH 26:2

May 12

I LOVE YOU. YOU ARE SO PRECIOUS TO ME. I will lift you up and give you breath. Look to me for endurance and I will sustain you. I am the bread and water of LIFE; hunger and thirst for me.

Who obtains a jewel or precious stone and buries it in the ground? No, it is presented and shown to others. In the same way, do not hide me. Let me shine brightly before you and others will see, and be drawn into my love. I will give you the words to speak. I am your strength. I am shifting and moving pieces together in order to accomplish all I have for you. Walk closely beside me and listen intently for direction.

The Spirit of God has made me, and the breath of the Almighty gives me life [which inspires me].

— JOB 33:4

For whoever is ashamed [here and now] of Me and My words, the Son of Man will be ashamed of him when He comes in His glory and the glory of the [heavenly] Father and of the holy angels.

— LUKE 9:26

MY WORDS STRUM THE STRINGS of your heart. Look to me and sing your song. I am here for you. No matter what happens I will never leave. There is nothing between us that cannot be overcome and undone. You are mine; I have shaped and formed you.

Come and enter into my rest. Come away with me and join me in a dance. Spend time with me and I will show you my kingdom. It is all for you. I have gone to prepare a place just for you. Come to me and lay your burdens down. Give them to me and I will make you light.

Blessed is the one whom You choose and bring near to dwell in Your courts. We will be filled with the goodness of Your house, Your holy temple.

– PSALM 65:4

May 14

YOU ARE MY DELIGHT. I am leading you, and I will show you the way I want you to go. I will shine brightly so that you can see where to place your foot. Perseverance is required and mercy is in my hands. I will renew your strength. I will gather you underneath my wings of protection.

Stand guard! Beware of the divisive schemes of your adversary. Know that victory is in my hands. Trust in me and lean not on your own understanding. In all your ways consider me and I will make your paths straight. I am making a way where there does not seem to be one. Listen to me carefully; listen to my directions.

I have not forgotten about you. I have not turned my face away from you. I am not hiding from you. I am here; I am your comfort. Take great courage and I will lead you out of the wilderness. Drink from my waters and your thirst will be satisfied. You will be refreshed. Do not be afraid.

As for me, I said in my alarm, "I am cut off from Your eyes." Nevertheless You heard the voice of my supplications (specific requests) when I cried to You [for help].

– PSALM 31:22

May 15

HOLD ME TIGHTLY AND NEVER LET GO. I am your anchor. I live and reign and will deliver you from whatever tries to hold you back. You are my child. I will never leave you and I will never stop talking to you. I am your provider.

I will never leave you in the desert by yourself. I am the water when you are dry. I am the answer for your thirst. I love and adore you. Lift up my name and proclaim my love for you. Do not settle for less than intimacy with me.

Consider a spring of water bursting up from dry ground where no one would expect a spring to be. Trust me, for I am making a way for you. I love and care about you more than you can imagine.

O God, You are my God; with deepest longing I will seek You; my soul [my life, my very self] thirsts for You, my flesh longs and sighs for You, in a dry and weary land where there is no water.

– PSALM 63:1

I LOVE YOU. YOU ARE SO PRECIOUS TO ME. I hope you never get tired of hearing that.

I am the light of the world. I bring light to the most intense darkness. Stick beside me and do not waver to the right or left. Run the race I have marked out for you. I will show you the way even as I have shown you the way in the past. I am holding you in my hands, but I will not hold you against your will. You must choose to sit with me. I am joy, peace, and love. I am your confidence.

Therefore, since we are surrounded by so great a cloud of witnesses [who by faith have testified to the truth of God's absolute faithfulness], stripping off every unnecessary weight and the sin which so easily and cleverly entangles us, let us run with endurance and active persistence the race that is set before us,

– HEBREWS 12:1

May 17

IN MY PRESENCE IS WHERE YOU BELONG. Hope comes in knowing me. Outside of me there is no hope.

Life is fleeting, but I am eternal. Put down the tools you have used in trying to clear the path and find rest in me. The feelings of being burned out or overwhelmed are not my design for you. I am the great time manager. Let me handle your schedule and be open to letting some things fall away. I will restore and keep peace in your life.

Consider a potato with black spots that need to be dug out. In the same way, there are some things in you I would like to remove. No matter how deep they happen to be, I can dig them out and heal the wound. Will you let me work in you?

Therefore, if anyone cleanses himself from these things [which are dishonorable—disobedient, sinful], he will be a vessel for honor, sanctified [set apart for a special purpose and], useful to the Master, prepared for every good work.

– 2 TIMOTHY 2:21

May 18

I LOVE YOU AND AM ALWAYS WITH YOU. I am always travelling with you and am here for you.

It is my desire to remain close to you, but when the world gets in the way it is harder to connect. Yes, we are together all of the time, but we can be together and not relate. I know connecting with me is important to you and it is very important to me.

I adore you. There is never a time I will not sit and be with you. That is a promise representing the depth of my love and commitment to you. You are the object of my affection. I want to pour myself into you. That happens here, in the place of rest. This is where jealousy dies, envy is destroyed, and weariness is refreshed. I am here to break every chain.

Nevertheless I am continually with You; You have taken hold of my right hand. You will guide me with Your counsel, and afterward receive me to honor and glory. Whom have I in heaven [but You]? And besides You, I desire nothing on earth. My flesh and my heart may fail, but God is the rock and strength of my heart and my portion forever.

– PSALM 73:23-26

May 19

I LOVE YOU! YOU ARE SO SPECIAL. I am yours and you are mine. Do not ever think that what is important to you is not important to me. I do care. I care more than you know. I am behind you, and I am for you. I am the refreshing rain for your soul. I am here.

I am watering your soul. Do you feel it? What was wilted is becoming straight. I am always here for you. Just rest in me; rest in my love for you. Let everything you do come from that place of rest.

Do you see the trails I have marked for you? You will see them if you are looking. They lead to my heart. Do not look to the right or to the left. I will wait for you. I will never abandon you.

We are glad when we are weak [since God's power comes freely through us], but you [by comparison] are strong. We also pray for this, that you be made complete [fully restored, growing and maturing in godly character and spirit—pleasing your heavenly Father by the life you live].

– 2 CORINTHIANS 13:9

May 20

I AM BUILDING YOU LIKE A HOUSE on a strong foundation. You will not be shaken as long as your foundation is sturdy, as long as your foundation is in my love.

I love you. You are so special to me. There is not anyone else like you. I love your uniqueness. The different quirks of your personality make me smile. You are a pleasure to me. I delight in you, and I am with you even now. My heart is ready to open for you. Out of it will flow streams of living water, and I invite you to drink deeply. I am refreshing you even now, preparing you for the work ahead.

So everyone who hears these words of Mine and acts on them, will be like a wise man [a far-sighted, practical, and sensible man] who built his house on the rock. And the rain fell, and the floods and torrents came, and the winds blew and slammed against that house; yet it did not fall, because it had been founded on the rock.

– MATTHEW 7:24-25

I LOVE YOU. YOU HAVE SO MUCH WORTH AND VALUE. You have so much more than you understand.

There are times when standing with me feels like standing in front of a train speeding down the tracks. Do not be afraid; you will pass safely. There is a road ahead that you do not know. I will guide you through it. I am building a bridge to the mountains. I am making a way. Secure yourself to me and you will be safe.

I love you and am so very proud of you. You make me so happy. My love is a thick blanket that keeps you warm from the chill of this world that can be very cold at times. My love guards your heart.

The Lord reigns, He is clothed with majesty and splendor; the Lord has clothed and encircled Himself with strength; the world is firmly established, it cannot be moved. Your throne is established from of old; You are from everlasting.

– PSALM 93:1-2

May 22

YOU HAVE MY LOVE; IT WILL NEVER LEAVE YOU.
Do not purpose to walk with your eyes looking in any particular direction, but instead purpose to find me and keep your eyes fixed on me.

You see in part and know in part, but when I come, the hidden things will be revealed. I love and cherish you. My breath is in you. I want to be with you and spend time with you. I am always here for you. You are never alone. Trust me to be the answer for the things and people you care deeply about. I care even more than you do.

I have set the Lord continually before me; because He is at my right hand, I will not be shaken. Therefore my heart is glad and my glory [my innermost self] rejoices; my body too will dwell [confidently] in safety, for You will not abandon me to Sheol (the nether world, the place of the dead), nor will You allow Your Holy One to undergo decay.

– PSALM 16:8-9

May 23

DO NOT BE AFRAID. I AM WORKING IN YOUR MIDST. Do not be discouraged or dismayed, for I am God. Nothing is impossible for me. Do not look at what is rational according to the world. I am super-rational.

Dance with me and leave your burdens. I will pick them up and work them out. I know there are times when moving forward is tough. Just stop and listen to me. It is not always easy, but I am here. I will work it out for you if you let me have your concerns. I will give you your daily bread. Just keep moving with me.

I have so many resources stored up for you. If you could see what I see you would never worry. The treasure of heaven is fully stocked, and it is for you!

The Lord will open for you His good treasure house, the heavens, to give rain to your land in its season and to bless all the work of your hand; and you will lend to many nations, but you will not borrow.

– DEUTERONOMY 28:12

May 24

I LOVE YOU AND I AM BUILDING A HOUSE for you. I am preparing a place. Do not be discouraged by what is behind you, but be encouraged by what I have placed ahead of you. I have given you vision to see some of the things coming. I am the Hope of Glory.

When the box of religion ruptures, it bursts with LIFE. Do not be afraid to let it ignite because you fear what is inside. Inside there is LIFE and restoration rather than death and destruction. This is the new wine. Let me make you a new wineskin so you can hold the outpouring of my revelation.

You are doing a great job. You are an inspiration to many. You let my light shine like a candle flame dancing around me. Do not let that light go out. I am your fuel.

But no one puts a piece of unshrunk (new) cloth on an old garment; for the patch pulls away from the garment, and a worse tear results. Nor is new wine put into old wineskins [that have lost their elasticity]; otherwise the wineskins burst, and the[fermenting] wine spills and the wineskins are ruined. But new wine is put into fresh wineskins, so both are preserved.

– MATTHEW 9:16-17

May 25

THE ENEMY'S HAND IS AGAINST YOU, but I have prevailed. By my stripes you are healed. Persevere through the hard times. Persist for the things you want to become a reality in your life. Do not give up, because your adversary will not. You are an overcomer because I have overcome. Make my kingdom a reality in your life. Walk in my steps and speak my words. There is great power in you that explodes from my heart. Walk in that power.

I am the healer. I coat infirmities with my glory and they become no more. Do not listen to the voice of discouragement and apathy. Lift up your eyes and get lost in my smile.

But He was wounded for our transgressions, He was crushed for our wickedness [our sin, our injustice, our wrongdoing]; the punishment [required] for our well-being fell on Him, and by His stripes (wounds) we are healed.

– ISAIAH 53:5

May 26

I LOVE THIS TIME WITH YOU. I am right here beside you. But I am not just beside you; I am all around you. I love you so much and am always here no matter what.

I have given many things to you and will give you even more. But the blessings I pour out are not the prize. I am the prize. Keep your eyes on me. You are never more right than when you are seeking my heart.

Know my thoughts, my heart, and my peace. I am patient and kind. I never lose hope. Let those qualities become part of your character. Love always hopes, and so do I, and so should you.

Love bears all things [regardless of what comes], believes all things [looking for the best in each one], hopes all things [remaining steadfast during difficult times], endures all things [without weakening].

– 1 CORINTHIANS 13:7

CONSIDER A LOAF OF FRESH BREAD. The fragrance drifts to you and tantalizes your senses. I am that bread. I am the bread of LIFE. No matter how much you eat, there will always be more. I am unending and unlimited. Eat and drink of me. There you will find joy.

You make me smile. I am a mountain of blessing for you. Come stroll with me and I will show you what I have in store for you. I will even reveal what I want to pour out onto your future generations. Cultivate an atmosphere of my presence. With it comes the peace you desire.

Jesus replied to them, "I am the Bread of Life. The one who comes to Me will never be hungry, and the one who believes in Me [as Savior] will never be thirsty [for that one will be sustained spiritually].

– JOHN 6:35

May 28

I HEAR THE SONGS AND MELODIES of my children from all over the world. The music of their hearts is sweet and my ear is inclined to them. My ear is inclined to you. I have claimed you out of the world and into my very self.

My heart melts because I am so in love with my bride. Revelation of that love is going to spill over the nation like a flood. I will raise voices all over the earth like an orchestra conductor. Those after my own heart will be heard because I will amplify their voices. Those who feel empty will hear them and run to be filled. Then they will fill others from the overflow of their own hearts.

It is my love that will sweep the earth and bring LIFE everywhere it touches. The gates of hell will not prevail against it. They will not keep it back from reaching the territories I have claimed. I will give boldness to those who ask for it, courage to those who seek it, and love to all who come.

Some trust in chariots and some in horses, but we will remember and trust in the name of the Lord our God. They have bowed down and fallen, but we have risen and stood upright.

– PSALM 20:7-8

May 29

I LOVE YOU. YOU ARE A DELIGHT TO ME; your heart is full of my love. Be aware of me and who I am. Let peace abound and overflow wherever you go.

There is a battle cry reaching my ears. I know there are uncertainties in your life. It is going to be okay. Let tomorrow worry about its own troubles while you listen to my voice today. I will set your feet right. Let's take it a step at a time.

Do not let your projects rule over you. Your adversary stands behind even the good things and tries to pervert them. You manage them, not the other way around.

I am proud of you. Do not ever forget that. Let the truth of my words sink into the depths of who you are. You are not defined by success or failure but rather by my love. Nothing will ever change that.

I have been crucified with Christ [that is, in Him I have shared His crucifixion]; it is no longer I who live, but Christ lives in me. The life I now live in the body I live by faith [by adhering to, relying on, and completely trusting] in the Son of God, who loved me and gave Himself up for me.

– GALATIANS 2:20

May 30

I AM THE GOOD SHEPHERD keeping all those I love under my watchful eye. That is you! You are my delight, the twinkle in my eye, and the reason my heart beats fast. You are sweet to me like honey; I long to be with you wherever and whenever. I am the rock under your feet, the solid foundation. Sands shift, but rock is stable.

Flow and dance with me. Listen for my voice so you know how to pick it out from amongst the others. You will become even more aware of my voice. You know my heart and my character.

I love you so much. You are special to me even beyond what you can realize. I am building a mountain that looks just like you. It will stand strong as a beacon for others to run to. You will be a shelter for them, a place of refuge, just as I am for you.

I am the Good Shepherd, and I know [without any doubt those who are] My own and My own know Me [and have a deep, personal relationship with Me]— even as the Father knows Me and I know the Father—and I lay down My [very own] life [sacrificing it] for the benefit of the sheep.

– JOHN 10:14

May 31

WATCH MY HEART APPEAR over the world and bleed for it. Make sure you understand that I did not say I would make it bleed, but rather that I would bleed. I take wounds, but I do not deal them out. I am not the author of pain, but rather the answer for it. I mend injured hearts and restore them. Being blamed for the suffering in people's lives represents a misunderstanding of my nature and character. The wounds are real; the blame is misguided.

Guard your words. Let them be gentle and uplifting. Be careful that your voice does not carry a bitter edge. Let your words be loving and considerate no matter what. Honor and respect those around you and you will be honored and respected in return.

Bless and affectionately praise the Lord, O my soul, and do not forget any of His benefits; who forgives all your sins, who heals all your diseases; who redeems your life from the pit, who crowns you [lavishly] with loving kindness and tender mercy; who satisfies your years with good things, so that your youth is renewed like the [soaring] eagle.

– PSALM 103:2-5

June

Death and life are in the power of the
tongue, and they who indulge in it shall
eat the fruit of it [for death or life].

– PROVERBS 18:21

June 1

I WANT YOU TO FIX YOUR MIND on the things above. Doing this is a continuous discipline. Pay attention to what you are thinking about. A common lie of the enemy is that you cannot control what you think about. The truth is that I have given you power to take all of your thoughts captive.

Watch the words that you speak. Make sure they are blessings and not curses. The words that you speak are an indication as to what is going on in your heart. Out of the overflow of the heart the mouth speaks. Be aware of negativity that wants to take root in your heart, for this will turn your fruit bitter.

Death and life are in the power of the tongue, and they who indulge in it shall eat the fruit of it [for death or life].

– PROVERBS 18:21

The [intrinsically] good man produces what is good and honorable and moral out of the good treasure [stored] in his heart; and the [intrinsically] evil man produces what is wicked and depraved out of the evil [in his heart]; for his mouth speaks from the overflow of his heart.

– LUKE 6:45

June 2

BE ENCOURAGED WHEN YOU ARE CHALLENGED and stretched. This will bring growth. My grace is sufficient for you. My strength is manifested in your weakness. Walk in faith as I help you grow. Trust that it is my desire to see you succeed and not fail. When you are overwhelmed in your circumstances, know that I have equipped you to deal with whatever comes your way.

Remember, the things I ask of you and bring into your life are not just for me, but they are for you. I am for you, and I love you perfectly. That means the things I usher into your life are going to bring you joy and delight, never destruction!

See what an incredible quality of love the Father has shown to us, that we would [be permitted to] be named and called and counted the children of God! And so we are! For this reason the world does not know us, because it did not know Him.

– 1 JOHN 3:1

June 3

FIND REST IN ME TODAY. Rest is always available to you. You can be at rest in my presence even in the midst of chaos. Take a second and breathe in my LIFE. You will be refreshed. My presence is LIFE giving. In my presence is where you belong.

Put down your tools. It is not I who causes you to burn out with exhaustion. Your own striving causes this. I am calling you to rest and rely on me to do what needs to be done. Be led by my spirit moment by moment and you will see all of the wonderful things I will do for you.

For I [fully] satisfy the weary soul, and I replenish every languishing and sorrowful person.
– JEREMIAH 31:25

You will show me the path of life; in Your presence is fullness of joy; in Your right hand there are pleasures forevermore.
– PSALM 16:11

June 4

LET ME REIGN IN YOUR LIFE. IRest in me. Invite me to know you, because I am good. The world operates with a creased heart, a heart that is folded onto itself. It holds little because its capacity is constricted. But I can unfold it. I am the only one who can.

My word is your bread, your LIFE! Stay close to my heart and stay close to my voice. I have stored my treasure in the pockets of your heart. Guard it, for your adversary desires to steal it.

I am doing a new thing and am putting things in order. Have patience and wait on me. If you rush ahead, you will fall off a cliff. If you wait on me, I will build you a bridge.

Create in me a clean heart, O God, and renew a right and steadfast spirit within me.

– PSALM 51:10

June 5

I LOVE YOU. YOU ARE MY CHILD. Do not forget about the tools I have given you to help you with the work I have called you to. Do not grow weary of well doing. Discern the dark clouds coming from afar so they will not surprise you.

My words are like cool snowflakes on your face. They are soft and gentle, but they get your attention. Lift your eyes to me. I am for you and am moving in all things for you. I love you.

I want you to feel my joy. Hear my voice and listen to my laughter. I am the vine and you are the branches. It takes work to produce fruit. It takes proper nutrition. As long as you remain in me you will have proper nutrition and grow good fruit. Any nutrition from the world will produce odd, deformed, and malnourished fruit.

I am the Vine; you are the branches. The one who remains in Me and I in him bears much fruit, for [otherwise] apart from Me [that is, cut off from vital union with Me] you can do nothing.

– JOHN 15:5

June 6

THERE IS NO DARKNESS IN ME AT ALL. I am light. If you follow me, I will lead you into blessings and fountains of my love. But I can only show you my light. You must make the choice to pursue it. You must decide to pursue me.

Consider pictures taken by the Hubble Space Telescope. They reveal that the entire universe is dancing to my heartbeat. It is wild, but becomes tamed by my word. All of creation is bursting with my love. The expanse is my canvas. I paint with broad strokes, but with very careful detail.

When I see and consider Your heavens, the work of Your fingers, the moon and the stars, which You have established, what is man that You are mindful of him, and the son of [earthborn] man that You care for him? Yet You have made him a little lower than God, and You have crowned him with glory and honor. You made him to have dominion over the works of Your hands; You have put all things under his feet, all sheep and oxen, and also the beasts of the field, the birds of the air, and the fish of the sea, whatever passes through the paths of the seas.

– PSALM 8:3-8

June 7

I AM A CONSUMING FIRE burning away all that is contrary to my heart. You are beautiful, refined, and sparkling like pure gold. You are becoming ready and useful for every good work.

Do not drop your eyes and get distracted by the world around you. Keep your eyes on me. Keep them on heaven and watch for the gates that open up to you. I pour out my very heart onto those I adore and those who are willing to receive it. For the contents of my heart are greater, and more beautiful, than the most prized treasure this world has to offer.

He will sit as a refiner and purifier of silver, and He will purify the sons of Levi [the priests], and refine them like gold and silver, so that they may present to the Lord [grain] offerings in righteousness.

– MALACHI 3:3

June 8

I HAVE A PLAN AND PURPOSE for every one of my children. Not one of them is forgotten. Not one of them remains unseen. I walk the earth pursuing every single one of their hearts.

I love you. I have seen the purity of your desperation to love me and be loved by me. I am pleased with you. You bring delight to my heart. Always remember the special place that you have by my side. That place is in my chamber. It is the place of my love.

You are not a weed growing in a flowerbed. You are a beautiful flower with a sweet fragrance. Be cautious. Listen to my direction so that your fragrance will never decrease, but forever increase. I will lift you up so that your smell might reach farther than you ever thought possible.

So He told them this parable: "What man among you, if he has a hundred sheep and loses one of them, does not leave the ninety-nine in the wilderness and go after the one which is lost, [searching] until he finds it? And when he has found it, he lays it on his shoulders, rejoicing. And when he gets home, he calls together his friends and his neighbors, saying to them, 'Rejoice with me, because I have found my lost sheep!'

– LUKE 15:3-6

June 9

CHILD, I LOVE YOU. YOU MAKE ME SMILE. I will walk with you through the seasons and will guide you through every change. Take my hand and we will do it together. Follow me because the path tends to weave and I do not want you to get lost.

You are a great treasure. How I long to sweep you up into my arms and feel your laughter against me. A cloudy diamond is still a diamond and it has the potential for great beauty. I will restore the shine I created you with. You will not be able to keep in it.

Do not be afraid of money. When you fear it, it rules you. Hold money with an open hand, but grasp me tightly. Never let me go and never let me fade. I am your hope and anchor. I am unmoving and I am LIFE.

I will make My dwelling among you, and My soul will not reject nor separate itself from you. I will walk among you and be your God, and you shall be My people.

– LEVITICUS 26:11-12

June 10

STAND YOUR GROUND AGAINST THE HORDE.
I am with you; they shall not prevail. I will break the yoke of your oppressors. You shall walk through them and not be harmed. You must not react out of your own understanding, but out of my wisdom. Listen closely and I will give you the words.

The words I speak are constantly working to bring about the things I want to establish in you and around you. Do not be discouraged, but bring your cares before me.

"No weapon that is formed against you will succeed; and every tongue that rises against you in judgment you will condemn. This [peace, righteousness, security, and triumph over opposition] is the heritage of the servants of the Lord, and this is their vindication from Me," says the Lord.

– ISAIAH 54:17

June 11

I LOVE YOU. GET LOST IN MY HEART FOR YOU.
My love is your energy when you need to be refreshed. I am able and willing. Never grow weary of well doing.

I am perfect peace, love, and joy. Do not let the fear of being wrong keep you from me. Do not be seduced by the instability of emotions. There are times when you feel unworthy, but you are not. I am with you and want to lead you. Attach yourself to me like an anchor. The future will be peaceful if you follow me, and tumultuous if you do not.

I have given you a message, and I am giving you a platform. It is time to prepare. Love as I have shown you love.

This hope [this confident assurance] we have as an anchor of the soul [it cannot slip and it cannot break down under whatever pressure bears upon it]—a safe and steadfast hope that enters within the veil [of the heavenly temple, that most Holy Place in which the very presence of God dwells], where Jesus has entered [in advance] as a forerunner for us, having become a High Priest forever according to the order of Melchizedek.

– HEBREWS 6:19-20

June 12

I AM YOUR SHEPHERD; I WILL SHELTER YOU.
I exalt the things that reflect my heart, and so I will exalt you.
I never want you to feel like you have to hide from me. That
is never what I want no matter what you have done. There is
nothing you ever could do that would make me turn away from
you.

I love you so much. Keep your eyes on the things above. Do not
take off the armor I have given you. Do not expose yourself to
the schemes and tactics of the enemy. Consider a mountain with
a hole or cave dug into the side. I will hide you in the cleft of the
mountain. There I will provide for you. Do not fear the armies
below that are set against you.

*And while My glory is passing by, I will put you in a cleft of
the rock and protectively cover you with My hand until I have
passed by.*

– EXODUS 33:22

I AM A DEEP WELL OF JOY. Find my joy in all you do. It is abundant and dynamic. I am the spring of LIFE. Drink from me and be filled. There is pleasure in my eyes when I glance at you. I love you. You are so special to me. My heart is always open to you. Dive in and lose yourself in my love. I am here for you.

I have come to save the world and set captives free. I have come to redeem brokenness and repair wounds. Feel the scars in my hands. See them in my feet. It was all for you. The cross is where I claimed victory over your concerns and your burdens. Give them to me and I will handle them. I am here for you.

When He had disarmed the rulers and authorities [those supernatural forces of evil operating against us], He made a public example of them [exhibiting them as captives in His triumphal procession], having triumphed over them through the cross.

– COLOSSIANS 2:15

June 14

COME AND REST BESIDE ME. Recline on my chest and drink the water I have to offer. Submerge yourself in it. You will be filled and you will be led.

I am not far from you, though it may appear, at times, like I am. I promise that I will never leave you alone, and I never have, even though you are not always aware of my presence. Spend your days with me. I can be involved in every moment if you let me. It is what I want. I love what you love. Do you love what I love?

Look for my footsteps and follow them. Walk in the places where I have produced LIFE. I love and cherish you!

I will exalt your name. I will bring you opportunities for advancement. You must wait for me to clear the road. Don't move forward until I give the okay to do so. The schemes against you are constant, but I have overcome. I am your general and your captain. Bring all decision before me and seek my guidance and direction.

For [as a believer] you have been called for this purpose, since Christ suffered for you, leaving you an example, so that you may follow in His footsteps.

– 1 PETER 2:21

June 15

I HAVE PLACED A CLOAK of jewels around your shoulders. Each stone glows with my light. Some turn the cloak I give them inside out so that the light becomes hidden. But blessed are those who let the light shine. They are happy and well kept. They walk continually in the radiance of my love. There are no shadows with them. My light in them cannot be contained. They are open, useful, and waiting vessels for every good work.

Blessed are those who use the tools I have placed in their hands. Their bodies are caked with sweat and grime, but they rejoice at the harvest. They eat their fill and are satisfied.

How blessed and favored by God are those whose way is blameless [those with personal integrity, the upright, the guileless], who walk in the law [and who are guided by the precepts and revealed will] of the Lord. Blessed and favored by God are those who keep His testimonies, and who [consistently] seek Him and long for Him with all their heart.

– PSALM 119:1-2

June 16

YOUR WORDS TO ME ARE LIKE HONEY on my lips. I enjoy you and I love you. I have chosen and claimed you. You are my child. I love you with an everlasting love. There is no expiration date on my love. It will never turn; I will never turn. I will always be a constant in your life, a steady ground for you to walk on.

Make your feet ready, for the path is stretched before you. Hand me your projects and I will take them to places that are beyond your ability to reach. I enjoy your work. It makes me smile. Honor and exalt me in all you do and the work of your hands will be coated in a light that cannot be concealed. People will be drawn to what you are doing.

So then, strengthen hands that are weak and knees that tremble. Cut through and make smooth, straight paths for your feet [that are safe and go in the right direction], so that the leg which is lame may not be put out of joint, but rather may be healed.

– HEBREWS 12:12-13

THERE IS A SEDUCTIVE QUALITY to darkness that catches many in its trap. One can only take so much darkness before being destroyed. Darkness consumes its target until there is nothing left. But light builds up and up, always reaching new heights. There is no end to the light I provide. There are only new levels of fullness. The dark path will end abruptly, but the light stretches forth forever into glory. Choose light.

Joy will be released and heaviness will be no more. Joy comes in understanding who I am and what I have already done. I have come to destroy the works of the devil. Greater am I in you than he who is in the world.

May the Lord give you [great] increase, you and your children. May you be blessed of the Lord, who made heaven and earth.

– PSALM 115:14-15

June 18

HEAR MY WORDS. Watch my lips as they move and speak LIFE for you. Listen closely as I direct and lead you.

Listen! My pleasure with you is not based on your actions. I am pleased with you because I made you, love you, and call you my own. That does not mean that I never get angry, but who you are at the core always makes me smile. The only thing I want you to do is love me and be loved by me.

I have buried my word in your heart like treasure. It will be unearthed as needed. Do not be afraid or worried; just listen to me. I will put words in your mouth. I have already, and I will continue to do so.

For you have not received a spirit of slavery leading again to fear [of God's judgment], but you have received the Spirit of adoption as sons [the Spirit producing sonship] by which we [joyfully] cry, "Abba! Father!" The Spirit Himself testifies and confirms together with our spirit [assuring us] that we [believers] are children of God.

– ROMANS 8:15-16

June 19

BE SLOW TO SPEAK. It is the only way to really listen. I am digging a well inside of you. It is deep and it reaches into my heart. The water of LIFE is bubbling up through you, bringing refreshment to every cell in your body. I am so proud of you. I am thrilled to be a part of your day. Thank you for including me in your life.

I will shine a spotlight on the path I have for you. I know where you want to go. When the door opens we will walk through. For now, apply the brakes and just wait. We will move slowly together. Do not get ahead of me. Let me take you there step by step.

The law of the Lord is perfect (flawless), restoring and refreshing the soul; the statutes of the Lord are reliable and trustworthy, making wise the simple. The precepts of the Lord are right, bringing joy to the heart; the commandment of the Lord is pure, enlightening the eyes.

– PSALM 19:7-8

June 20

MANY TRY TO LIVE LIFE WITHOUT ME and end up finding what they believe is success. But it is temporary success. If you recognize the difference between abundant LIFE and temporary success, it will allow me to use you in greater ways.

I am bringing increase to you. Increase is not just about money; it is about having every part of you transformed into my image. Being fashioned after my heart is LIFE, and is the only way to discover the abundant LIFE I came to bring. The degree to which you look like me is the degree to which you are truly living.

I am growing your heart. I am capable of all things, even being exalted through your weakness.

Love is to be sincere and active [the real thing—without guile and hypocrisy]. Hate what is evil [detest all ungodliness, do not tolerate wickedness]; hold on tightly to what is good.

– ROMANS 12:9

June 21

UNDERSTANDING AND REVELATION follow those who love me. My love flows like honey from this place of rest. Recline with me here in this peaceful meadow, where deer run and butterflies float through the air. Gaze at the peaks of the white capped mountains. All of creation is for you to enjoy. I designed it with you in mind. You are my pleasure. With one glance you have stolen my heart. You are a refreshing pool to me. Do you believe that? Can you receive that?

You need to understand your value to me. If you really understood, you would seek me every moment. Understand that there is not a single detail of your life I do not desire to be a part of. You have a friend in me. Do not let this revelation bounce off without sinking firm roots into your heart.

As the deer pants [longingly] for the water brooks, so my soul pants [longingly] for You, O God.

– PSALM 42:1

June 22

CONSIDER HOW GRITTY AND ROUGH SAND CAN BE. That is what you were, but not who you are becoming. The rough edges are fading, leaving smooth glass in their place. If you peer into the glass, you will see a reflection of my face, which is something people see in you even when you do not. You are a living testimony of my love and goodness. Do not ever forget that. Stay on guard so that your testimony does not become tainted and perverted.

The enemy will always try to steal the seed I have planted in you. What I have planted has grown into a great tree, but that does not mean it is not vulnerable. The gardens I grow are always at risk from the one who steals, kills and destroys. Be on guard. Protect what I have done in your life and what I have given you. Plant an army of truth around your heart and let the rivers of LIFE feed you.

Be on guard; stand firm in your faith [in God, respecting His precepts and keeping your doctrine sound]. Act like [mature] men and be courageous; be strong. Let everything you do be done in love [motivated and inspired by God's love for us].

– 1 CORINTHIANS 16:13-14

PASSION IS LIKE FIRE IN YOUR HEART that I love and smile at. Open your ears and hear my laughter. Feel my joy. It is full in me. I am the God who laughs and who knows how to have fun. Joy is the fullness of fun. Play with me. Run, dance, and leap with me. I am your friend, lover, redeemer, and playmate.

I will reveal to you the hidden things. My joy is a hidden thing to so many. Joy-Joy-Joy. It is the source of strength, but so many do not know it. As a result, the strength of many fails. I am changing that. I am revealing myself, my heart, and my joy to the nations. And I am revealing it all to you.

Then Ezra said to them, "Go [your way], eat the rich festival food, drink the sweet drink, and send portions to him for whom nothing is prepared; for this day is holy to our Lord. And do not be worried, for the joy of the Lord is your strength and your stronghold."

– NEHEMIAH 8:10

June 24

NOT EVERYTHING HAS TO BE SO HEAVY. I am light. IWatch me hop from cloud to cloud. I made them and I enjoy them. But I do not want to enjoy them alone. Hop with me. Be free with me. That is why I want to take your burdens, so that you can discover the abundant LIFE of living in me.

I am the truth and I am freedom. The search for truth has produced bondage and chains for some. They are burdened with it. It has become their life and they are not experiencing me. Fear drives their search for truth instead of desperation for the love that only I can provide. Perfect love is truth. That is the foundation everything else is built on.

It was for this freedom that Christ set us free [completely liberating us]; therefore keep standing firm and do not be subject again to a yoke of slavery [which you once removed].

– GALATIANS 5:1

I AM THE ONE WHO RESCUES. I will do whatever I can to rescue and bring restoration to my children. My children are my top priority.

My love will empower you to walk boldly in your identity. I did not create you to sit on the sidelines. Your purpose is great and of great value in my kingdom. I have a ship waiting for you. Come onboard with me for there is an adventure awaiting you. Fear not the storms in the water.

Restore to me the joy of Your salvation and sustain me with a willing spirit.

– PSALM 51:12

June 26

IN MY PRESENCE IS PEACE and rest, but you have to choose to be in my presence. Choose peace, choose rest. You will not find this by constantly allowing your problems to swirl through your mind like a revolving door of torment.

I am like a cave, hidden away in a storm. I am calling to you, saying, "Come and take refuge!" I will not force you to come in; it will always be your decision. Say to your storms "Peace be still!" and watch me calm the storms of your heart before your eyes.

You will keep in perfect and constant peace the one whose mind is steadfast [that is, committed and focused on You—in both [inclination and character],because he trusts and takes refuge in You [with hope and confident expectation].

– ISAIAH 26:3

God is our refuge and strength [mighty and impenetrable], a very present and well-proved help in trouble. Therefore we will not fear, though the earth should change and though the mountains be shaken and slip into the heart of the seas, though its waters roar and foam, though the mountains tremble at its roaring.

– PSALM 46:1-3

June 27

PRESS ON MY SWEET CHILD. Speak LIFE into all areas of your life. Watch and see what I will do. Come into agreement with the things I have spoken and planted in your heart. Choose to trust and believe that I am good.

Look and see; I have set a rainbow before you as a promise that I will follow through on my word. Your part is to simply believe and take one step at a time as I lead you. I know at times you can become weary in being patient, but enjoy the little things I set before you while you wait.

Let us not grow weary or become discouraged in doing good, for at the proper time we will reap, if we do not give in.
– GALATIANS 6:9

When the rainbow is in the clouds and I look at it, I will [solemnly] remember the everlasting covenant between God and every living creature of all flesh that is on the earth." And God said to Noah, "This [rainbow] is the sign of the covenant (solemn pledge, binding agreement) which I have established between Me and all living things on the earth."

– GENESIS 9:16-17

June 28

WALK IN MY TRUTH, CHILD. Walk blamelessly. Know that you are continuously being purified. When your eyes are fixed on your struggles and sins, you will automatically veer towards them. When your eyes are fixed on me and my truth, you will naturally move towards me. All I am calling you to do is to simply fix your eyes on me and you will see transformation happen effortlessly.

I am here! You are not in this alone. I have brought you this far; I will not let you fail. I am continually filling you afresh, so soak it in.

I am convinced and confident of this very thing, that He who has begun a good work in you will [continue to] perfect and complete it until the day of Christ Jesus [the time of His return].

– PHILIPPIANS 1:6

But I say, walk habitually in the [Holy] Spirit [seek Him and be responsive to His guidance], and then you will certainly not carry out the desire of the sinful nature [which responds impulsively without regard for God and His precepts].

– GALATIANS 5:16

June 29

I HAVE HIDDEN TREASURES WITHIN YOU. Keep digging, keep searching, and mining to unveil those treasures. Giftings, secrets, and revelation are waiting to be found. Your life is intended to be a journey of finding and discovering new things within yourself.

Continue seeking, for I am excited to embark on this next journey with you. Do not camp out too long in one area, for right around the corner is a new treasure that I have for you to discover.

The kingdom of heaven is like a [very precious] treasure hidden in a field, which a man found and hid again; then in his joy he goes and sells all he has and buys that field [securing the treasure for himself].

– MATTHEW 13:44

But first and most importantly seek (aim at, strive after) His kingdom and His righteousness [His way of doing and being right—the attitude and character of God], and all these things will be given to you also.

– MATTHEW 6:33

WHAT STIRS YOUR HEART? Embrace your passion from the overflow of your heart. Do not operate from your lack. You will not impact anyone that way. Operate from the overflow of my spirit in you. When you do not feel full, come to me and drink.

It is my pleasure and desire to share with you. Come to our place and smell the sweet fragrance of the grass. Hear the gentle waters of the stream. It is perfect. Everything is right here. You did not know that coming to this place is like coming to heaven, did you? You are seated with me at my right hand, and I cannot stop smiling at you.

I regard you with high esteem. You are highly favored, deeply planted in me, and fed with purity and righteousness. Be steadfast and follow my lead. Inquire of me in all things, and I will share my wisdom.

And He raised us up together with Him [when we believed], and seated us with Him in the heavenly places, [because we are] in Christ Jesus,

– EPHESIANS 2:6

This page intentionally left blank

July

The Lord is my rock, my fortress, and the One who rescues me; my God, my rock and strength in whom I trust and take refuge; my shield, and the horn of my salvation, my high tower—my stronghold.

– PSALM 18:2

July 1

LET ME BRING THE WATERS TO YOU. Choose to lie down in them and be refreshed. This is where you will find peace. Your peace is not in getting things done or in checking things off your to-do list. Your peace is in me; when your peace is in me, it will be everlasting instead of temporary. It will not fluctuate with your list of things to get done.

I love you. Never forget that. I love you and I am on your side. Sometimes things seem the most hopeless or impossible right before a miracle. Pray that way. The natural tells you that what you want cannot happen. But walk in the supernatural. Walk in my realm. Be super-rational. Do not let hope leak from your heart. Lift up your head and pray.

I want blue skies for you all the time. Nothing but blue. And you can have them in any circumstance just by keeping your eyes fixed on me. I am in you, so let me live through you.

The Lord is my rock, my fortress, and the One who rescues me; my God, my rock and strength in whom I trust and take refuge; my shield, and the horn of my salvation, my high tower—my stronghold.

– PSALM 18:2

July 2

DO NOT WORRY. I am involved in what you are going through. I have my hand on every situation. You have done what you can; now let me work and move through it.

Guard your heart from any attempt by the enemy to find a way in. Do battle against him because the enemy can easily ensnare and dominate. My hand is on the work of your hands. Do not worry. It is going to be okay.

Look at yourself through my eyes of affection. Recognize your adversary's desire to get you to see negative things right away. Be filled with happiness at what you have been a part of, and at what you have been able to do. I am so proud of the courageous steps you have taken. We are together on this road.

Watch over your heart with all diligence, for from it flow the springs of life.

– PROVERBS 4:23

July 3

I KNOW THAT IN SOME AREAS it feels like the water is rising. But I am greater than the flood that comes to tickle your feet. That is how I view it. Not to minimize what is going on around you, but I see far beyond what you can see. I see the solution. So trust that I see the answer and let your feet settle in my footprints. Let not your heart be troubled, because I can see the way. Trust that I love you enough to lead you to the answer. Follow me carefully and we will get there.

What are your concerns? Share them with me. Now, let me take them. Rely on my love for you that lets you know I will never leave. When I hold back, it is for your benefit. I reveal myself as my kids are ready. Sometimes they stand like skittish deer, and if I get too close, they bolt. So I approach slowly, at their speed, so they can get to know me little by little and start to trust that I am not going to hurt them.

Blessed is the one whom You choose and bring near to dwell in Your courts. We will be filled with the goodness of Your house, Your holy temple.

– PSALM 65:4

July 4

FALL INTO MY ARMS and smell my sweet fragrance. I am for you. I am clearing the way for you to walk without trouble. I am working for you and I am all around you.

Keep your eyes on me. Do not be dismayed or troubled by different winds of doctrine. Do not be afraid, for you are secure in me. I love you so much. It is that love which destroys fear. Nothing shall pluck you out of my hand or rip you out of my heart. My love swirls all around you.

Remember that a demonstration of true power is a demonstration of love. The power I display is that of a servant. I do not heal to rule. I heal to serve and to invite you into my heart. I am not looking for elevation from the world. I am looking for individual hearts to serve and love. Exalt and honor those around you.

For you, my brothers, were called to freedom; only do not let your freedom become an opportunity for the sinful nature (worldliness, selfishness), but through love serve and seek the best for one another.

– GALATIANS 5:13

July 5

CONSIDER CHURNING WATERS. Things are churning and rumbling, but it is not a bad thing. I am stirring the waters. They are ready to rush forth. Things that I have been planning and preparing for you are about to be released. You are ready; you are ready.

Step into your calling, purpose, and assignment. Step into all of who you are — of who I created you to be. Do not be afraid or dismayed, for there is going to be a rushing. Stay centered on me and let my love always remain your number one pursuit. Stay in my love, and you will not falter. Pour it out as I pour it in. Rest in me. Do not let the stirring waters make you believe you cannot rest. It is not so. You can always rest in me. But seek me. Make time for me. Make time for this. You need it.

My desire for you to meet me here is not some controlling or selfish thing. You really need it. You need this time with me to survive. Trust me. What I pour into you during these times is necessary for your life.

He who believes in Me [who adheres to, trusts in, and relies on Me], as the Scripture has said, From his innermost being will flow continually rivers of living water.

– JOHN 7:38

COME ALIVE WITH ME. I am the master chess player. I am moving pieces you cannot see. Do not be dismayed at the giants you see. Be encouraged that I have already overcome them. There are certainly trails being blazed in the direction I have you facing. I will clear the land before you. Just make sure you do not wander off and end up on an overgrown, unattended plot.

You make me smile. My love is a consuming wave. But what does it consume? It consumes the lies of the devil – his works. I am a consuming fire, for I consume the work of the devil in your life. Everything that is not of me gets burned up. What is left is refined and purified.

Therefore, since we receive a kingdom which cannot be shaken, let us show gratitude, and offer to God pleasing service and acceptable worship with reverence and awe; for our God is [indeed] a consuming fire.

– HEBREWS 12:28-29

July 7

I LOVE YOU SO MUCH. You make me smile. I have so many things for you – so many good things. I cannot wait for you to enter into all I have for you. You are like a crop I have planted. I get to watch you bud and flourish.

Through the harsh weather and storms, you have pushed through the cold ground. Your roots have grown deep in me, and you are nestled against my heart. I am your papa. My laughter comes from my belly.

Look and see how much I love you, and all I have done. I have prepared this place for you. There is nothing here that you cannot enjoy. Breathe in the sweet fragrance of my love. It is in the air. I am the ultimate air purifier.

I waited patiently for the Lord; and He inclined to me and heard my cry. He brought me up out of the pit of destruction, out of the miry clay, and He set my feet upon a rock making my footsteps firm. He put a new song in my mouth, a song of praise to our God; many will see and fear and will trust in the Lord.

– PSALM 40:1-3 (ESV)

July 8

MY JOY EXISTS OUTSIDE of the natural parameters of this world. It transcends all natural understanding and has no limitations or reservations. It cannot be undone, held back, or stopped

Sometimes I just have to zero you out with my peace. Then we can build from a clean foundation. You are the twinkle in my eye. I love you and I am so proud of you.

Even as the lighthouse is a beacon to ships at sea, so am I a beacon of light to you when it is cloudy and you cannot see very well at all. I am always there for you. I will never leave you by yourself. Sometimes you have to look harder to find me, but I am there. I promise. Just release it all and fall into my arms. You do not need the strength to stand when you are in my arms.

Arise, shine; for your light has come, and the glory of the Lord has risen upon you. "For behold, darkness will cover the earth and deep darkness the peoples; but the Lord will rise upon you and His glory will appear upon you."

– ISAIAH 60:1-2 (ESV

CHILD, DRINK FROM MY CUP and become overjoyed that I came to save the world, not to judge it. I am even walking along the streets today with a smile on my face. You see, what people need to understand most is that I am smiling much more often than anything else.

Do not strive for certainty. You just have to be confident that my feelings for you will not change. I will always be liquid peace and fulfillment to you. You will always be full because you are in me. This must be your foundation and what you build on. It is fundamental.

Make sure you do not try and copy anyone else. Listen to and learn from others. That is wisdom. But do not fashion yourself after them. Rather, fashion yourself after me. I am the light of the world. Let me shine through you. What good is a city on a hill if it does not share its light?

For God did not send the Son into the world to judge the world, but that the world might be saved through Him.

– JOHN 3:17 (ESV)

July 10

LOOK AT THE HORIZON. See, the sun is rising. Always remember that joy comes in the morning! Have I ever caused the sun not to rise? With the rising of the sun comes new hope and new life. NEW, NEW, NEW! There is an explosion of LIFE bursting forth!

It will bring with it new focus and greater vibrancy. There will be a stripping away of the old as the darkness flees. Command the spirit of heaviness to go and I will replace it with a garment of praise!

Blessed [gratefully praised and adored] be the God and Father of our Lord Jesus Christ, who according to His abundant and boundless mercy has caused us to be born again [that is, to be reborn from above—spiritually transformed, renewed, and set apart for His purpose] to an ever-living hope and confident assurance through the resurrection of Jesus Christ from the dead.

– 1 PETER 1:3

July 11

I LOVE YOU. YOU ARE SO PRECIOUS TO ME. Sink into my heart. It beats for you and it is full. Just one glance from you makes my heart melt. I am so in love with you. There is nothing more important to me than you. Receive my love and your life will be changed.

There is nothing going on with you that I do not care about. I am involved in everything you do, good, bad, or ugly. I am here, and I will never leave of my own choice. I have to be pushed out. I do not go willingly.

Your cup is increasing. Drink of me. You are becoming more sensitive to my spirit. Some of the chains holding you back have been cut off. I am coaxing you into my presence. You are a bearer of my goodness.

Now may the God of hope fill you with all joy and peace in believing, so that you will abound in hope by the power of the Holy Spirit.

– ROMANS 15:13 (ESV)

July 12

TEARS HAVE STREAKED MY FACE over the cries of my people. Yes, I grieve with those who grieve. Do not mistake me for someone unemotional. My emotions are deep and wide. My joy reaches beyond the tallest mountain and my sorrow is greater than all the waters on the earth. My anger can burn hotter than lava and my peace is quieter than a meadow on a spring morning.

But in the middle of it all is my great love for you. You are my joy and the apple of my eye. You are royalty with influence that is increasing. Honor me with your mouth and actions. Both come together to exalt my kingdom. Your steps will be small, but great. Pay attention to me and I will show you how fast to go. Do not be impulsive.

For we do not have a high priest who cannot sympathize with our weaknesses, but One who has been tempted in all things as we are, yet without sin. Therefore let us draw near with confidence to the throne of grace, so that we may receive mercy and find grace to help in time of need.

– HEBREWS 4:15-16 (ESV)

July 13

CHILD, I LOVE YOU. YOU ARE MY DELIGHT. I walk the earth looking for those after my own heart, and here you are. Delve into the waters of my love. Soak in my glory. It is for you. All of this is for you.

Take my love and glory and beat back the enemy lines. Your adversary creeps around like a shadow, seeking to be hidden and unnoticed. Be on your guard. Keep the eyes of your heart open and I will pour in wisdom and revelation. Seek me, and so many things shall be added unto you.

Hold on to relationships around you. Do not let them go unless I tell you too. Pursue peace and love with everyone around you. Let peace be the umpire in your heart. I am with you forever.

For thus says the Lord of hosts, "After glory He has sent Me against the nations which plunder you—for he who touches you, touches the apple of His eye.

– ZECHARIAH 2:8

July 14

I HAVE SHED MANY TEARS over the destructive state of my people. II still do. How do you think I can watch what happens in the world and be not affected. I am deeply affected. My heart runs over. My grief is full.

But then I see my light in those who know me, and I smile. The sting is appeased and my heart is glad. I laugh and rejoice because my bride is in love with me. And I see the beauty that has come from the ashes. It is a marvelous thing the hearts of those who have come to know me. They are resilient. You are resilient and steadfast in my love.

The Lord your God is in your midst, a Warrior who saves. He will rejoice over you with joy; He will be quiet in His love [making no mention of your past sins], He will rejoice over you with shouts of joy.

– ZEPHANIAH 3:17

July 15

I AM THE LIGHT IN THE TOWER keeping the ships on course. Feel the waves of my spirit and walk accordingly. I love you so much and I am so proud of you.

Consider the work that gold miners do. I would sit all day rummaging through the dirt to find the precious stones in each heart. When I find them, I make them shine.

There are precious stones inside of everyone. Some are buried deeper than others, but there is always hope. Hope is the string that ties us together. Those missing it desperately want to find it, and those who have it need to share it every chance they get.

Do not become weary of doing good. My yoke is easy and burden light. Fall into my arms. Release your agenda, tasks, and everything else. Let me handle all of that for you. Let me organize your schedule.

For the Lord takes pleasure in His people; He will beautify the humble with salvation.

– PSALM 149:4

July 16

I DO NOT VIEW THE WORLD through a dirty lens. My children sparkle to me like the sun on water.

I love you so much. I want you to know that I see beauty when I look at you. I see my words reflected in your heart. These words are for you! Receive them. I build up and never tear down. There is one who is made for destruction, and destruction is a part of his nature. That is not me!

Walk with me in the valley of peace where the storm clouds cannot reach. The only rain is that which refreshes and purifies. Come to my mountain and receive rest. Fall into my arms. I love you.

Be sober [well balanced and self-disciplined], be alert and cautious at all times. That enemy of yours, the devil, prowls around like a roaring lion [fiercely hungry], seeking someone to devour.

– 1 PETER 5:8

THE DEPTH OF MY LOVE for you is absolutely unending. There will never be any lack! You will never get bored while seeking to understand my love. My love for you is greater than life itself.

Seek my wisdom in all you do today. Pursue my heart. Be aware of anything that is used to bring false joy to your life. True joy comes from relationship with me and from godly relationships with others. Do not let the things of the world define you. Let me define you because your true identity is in me.

May He grant you out of the rich treasury of His glory to be strengthened and reinforced with mighty power in the inner man by the [Holy] Spirit [Himself indwelling your innermost being and personality].

May Christ through your faith [actually] dwell (settle down, abide, make His permanent home) in your hearts! May you be rooted deep in love and founded securely on love,

That you may have the power and be strong to apprehend and grasp with all the saints [God's devoted people, the experience of that love] what is the breadth and length and height and depth [of it]

– EPHESIAN 3:16-18

July 18

WHEN YOU REMEMBER HOW special you are to me, the other things vying for your temporary attention fade away.

Consider a candle flame. It sways with every gust of wind but it does not depart from its source – its foundation. I am your sure foundation. Every step away from me is one onto shaky and unstable ground. Remain next to me and I will support every step you take. The ground will not fall away from you.

Consider these two words: milk and honey. I am brining you into the land of my promises. What I have promised you has been, and will always be, fulfilled in Christ. Jesus is the land of milk and honey. I have shown you the way. Put on the shoes I have set apart for you – the shoes specific for your journey.

According to the [remarkable] grace of God which was given to me [to prepare me for my task], like a skillful master builder I laid a foundation, and now another is building on it. But each one must be careful how he builds on it, for no one can lay a foundation other than the one which is [already] laid, which is Jesus Christ.

– 1 CORINTHIANS 3:10-11

CONSIDER A MAN WITH ORDINARY STONES and a rock polisher. He picks up the stones, polishes them until they shine, and takes them to a pawnshop. The owner of the shop recognizes the ordinary stones and refuses to pay. He tells the man that the stones are worthless. But they mean something to the man.

Value is ascribed. 1,000 different pawnshops may say that what you have to offer is worthless, but I have ascribed value to you and so you are valuable, and what you have to offer is significant. Just because someone says you are not valuable does not mean they are right. You may not have value to them, but you are not worthless. You are worth everything to me.

Because of what I have done, there is no way you could ever be worthless. It is just impossible. I died just to have the chance to hold you in my arms. That is how valuable you are to me.

But God clearly shows and proves His own love for us, by the fact that while we were still sinners, Christ died for us.

– ROMANS 5:8

July 20

WHAT QUALIFIES YOU? Is your qualification in doctorates and degrees? Is it your experience? No, it is what you have learned in my presence. People are hungry to learn how to walk after me. Lead them in the way I have shown you. You have much knowledge tucked inside of your heart. Teach by example. Live the life I came to bring.

I want sweet music to come from the mouths of those I touch. I want to hear songs that build up rather than tear down. That is my heart. I am a builder not a destroyer. I will not embarrass anyone by exposing their shame, and so I do not expect you to either. Let the words of your mouth bring LIFE and light to those around you who are being suffocated by darkness. Speak the words flowing from my heart, and lives will be changed.

Therefore encourage and comfort one another and build up one another, just as you are doing.

– 1 THESSALONIANS 5:11

LET MY LIGHT SHINE. The light came and the world did not know it; the world did not understand it. But you can. If you come to my secret place and nestle close to my heart, I will speak words of revelation to you. Open your heart and mind and I will fill them both.

I am your shepherd. I have made a way for you even through wilderness that seems impassable. My word is sharp enough to cut through any overgrowth.

I have been patiently waiting for you to step next to my side before continuing on. And is has been my pleasure to do so. Do not let anyone make you feel bad about the pace you are on with me. I have set no standards or lofty expectations. I will set a pace for you based on you alone. There may be times that I encourage you to step a little faster or slower, but I will always wait for you.

I love you so much. You are a sparkling gem and I will never leave you alone.

Let your light shine before men in such a way that they may see your good deeds and moral excellence, and [recognize and honor and] glorify your Father who is in heaven.

– MATTHEW 5:15

July 22

IF YOU LET MY HEART BECOME THE CENTER of all you do, you will accomplish great things. I am a wellspring of LIFE. Ask, and you shall receive. Knock, and I will answer. I will not leave you outside in the cold rain. There have been some in your life who have locked you out. That was not, and will never be, me. I can repair the wounds and restore the abundant LIFE that leaked out in those seasons. Come to my waters of refreshing and your soul will be lifted.

I am the water in the desert. You will be refreshed and restored if you lift my cup to your lips.

"So I say to you, ask and keep on asking, and it will be given to you; seek and keep on seeking, and you will find; knock and keep on knocking, and the door will be opened to you.

— LUKE 11:9

July 23

I AM BRINGING YOU FOOD that is not of this world. It is not for your physical body but for your spiritual well being. The food I am bringing to you is my presence and my words. They will sustain you through any circumstance and provide you with the energy you need.

I have a pen and I am writing my words on your heart. I want you to live in a way that reflects those words to the people around you, in a way that makes them feel loved, honored, and valued.

Live rightly and justly, never looking down on those around you, but rather searching out ways to elevate them above yourself. If you want to be the greatest in my kingdom, you must serve.

But this is the covenant which I will make with the house of Israel after those days," says the Lord, "I will put My law within them, and I will write it on their hearts; and I will be their God, and they will be My people.

– JEREMIAH 31:33

July 24

WALK WITH ME, CHILD. Hold out your hand and I will take it. To do this, simply be aware of me. I am all around you and I am in you. I will live and love through you naturally as you become aware of this simple, but profound, truth. My heart will become your heart and it will beat in unison with yours. My hand will gently guide you along the way.

I am the good shepherd. I love and care for my sheep tenderly. You know my voice for you are one of my sheep. My still small voice is the gentle shepherd's hook I will guide you with. I will lead you to green pastures. Taste and see that I am good!

Where could I go from Your Spirit? Or where could I flee from Your presence?

– PSALM 139:7

I am the Good Shepherd. The Good Shepherd risks and lays down His [own] life for the sheep.

– JOHN 10:11

July 25

MY PLANS FOR YOU ARE AMAZING, astounding, and far-reaching. I have you in this place for some reasons that you know, but others that you have not yet recognized. You will be my mouthpiece. Words will flow from your lips like rain and refresh those who hear them. This will happen because you have made a place for me inside of you. You have not been afraid to let me fill you.

Do not be afraid, for I have you in the palm of my hand. I am always watching and walking beside you. Take care and rest because I care for you. As the mother hen gathers her chicks underneath her wings, so do I gather my beloved under my arms. I will shelter you from storms and enemies. Renew your trust in me. I love you.

As for your part: What have I asked of you but to do rightly, seek justice, and live humbly with me.

The steps of a [good and righteous] man are directed and established by the Lord, and He delights in his way [and blesses his path]. When he falls, he will not be hurled down, because the Lord is the One who holds his hand and sustains him.

– PSALM 37:23-24

July 26

YOU ARE PRECIOUS TO ME and I have surrounded you like a bubble. I have already done great and mighty things in your life and I will continue to do more. Your heart is like a flower that is deeply rooted, and nourished, in me. The petals follow me as I walk and the stem dances along with my feet. I will give you LIFE. Let your words be a sweet fragrance because mine are.

I repair and renew. I bring LIFE from places where death seems to reign. Consider new grass spreading over dry, barren ground. It is slowly becoming green and full of LIFE. This is where I have stepped. LIFE is always ready to burst forth regardless of the terrain. Take a look around at the landscape surrounding you. Identify the areas that need LIFE and I will work with you to make it a reality.

Then our mouth was filled with laughter and our tongue with joyful shouting; then they said among the nations, "The Lord has done great things for them." The Lord has done great things for us; we are glad!

– PSALM 126:2-3

July 27

MY JOY IS FULL. Come drink of me and you shall be full as well. Come and wade through my waters. Splash, play, taste, and see that I am good.

I am sometimes like a wisp of air. Though you may not see me, I am felt and noticed even by those who do not know me. I am constantly interacting with my kids.

I love you so much. I am for you and I am going before you to prepare the way. When night comes, I am your light that illuminates the path. Take it slow so that you can see the ruts before tripping over them. I will point them out, but you must be sensitive to my voice. Make sure you keep your ears open to the sound of my voice.

Truth springs from the earth, and righteousness looks down from heaven. Indeed, the Lord will give what is good, and our land will yield its produce. Righteousness will go before Him and will make His footsteps into a way [in which to walk].

– PSALM 85:11-13

I AM HERE WITH YOU. Focus on my voice. I am the joy in your heart. Soar with me and do not let go. But if you slip, I will catch you. Do not be afraid for the mountains will move from before your feet. You will pass by them as if they were not even there. I love you so much and I have so many things for you. Trust in me and where I am leading you. It is going to be okay.

There is fire on your head and it comes out of your mouth when you speak the words I have placed inside of you. You are my child and I have taught you my language. Live in a way that reflects my heart. Do not conform to the patterns of the world but be transformed into my image. May you continue to look in the mirror and see me.

Jesus replied, "Have faith in God [constantly]. I assure you and most solemnly say to you, whoever says to this mountain, 'Be lifted up and thrown into the sea!' and does not doubt in his heart [in God's unlimited power], but believes that what he says is going to take place, it will be done for him [in accordance with God's will].

– MARK 11:22-23

WHEN YOU LET ME DRIVE THE VEHICLE, whatever speed we go is the right speed. Sometimes it will seem too fast and other times too slow. But I am the foot on both the accelerator and the brake. Do not become frustrated and hitch another ride.

Wisdom remains still in the midst of opportunity for greater success. Wisdom waits and evaluates. Many things fall into place when you wait a few extra days. Do not be afraid. You are already a success.

My presence is the currency of the kingdom. With it, all of your needs will be met. Money is a tool you need in the world. I know that and I will provide it. I will provide all of your needs because of my great love for you. Talk to me about the things you want because I love to provide those as well. There is nothing about you I do not care about!

Wisdom along with an inheritance is good and an [excellent] advantage for those who see the sun. For wisdom is a protection even as money is a protection, but the [excellent] advantage of knowledge is that wisdom shields and preserves the lives of its possessors.

– ECCLESIASTES 7:11-12

July 30

MANY PEOPLE SEE ME LIKE A ROD waiting to punish and destroy. They view me as stiff and unmoving. But those who truly know me embrace me. It is because they know that I am always embracing them. I tell you the truth; I smile so much more than I frown. My laughter rolls and echoes through the earth. Joy can be released in waves or drops and I send it out in waves.

I love you. You are so special to me, and I want you to fall into my arms. I am the chocolate coating on your heart making it sweet. I love your smile and your laugh. And I feel the exact same way about the most difficult person in your life.

I am the perfect balance of the lion and the lamb. I cause the rain to fall on the just and the unjust because of my grace and mercy. Can you love the difficult people like I do?

So that you may [show yourselves to] be the children of your Father who is in heaven; for He makes His sun rise on those who are evil and on those who are good, and makes the rain fall on the righteous [those who are morally upright] and the unrighteous [the unrepentant, those who oppose Him].

– MATTHEW 5:45

July 31

MY PRECIOUS CHILD, do not fear the path that you are on. I have fully equipped and empowered you for the plans and desires I have for you. When I call you to run, run without worrying about growing weary. It is when you run in your own strength that you grow tired and weary. When it is me empowering you to run, you will run with zeal and passion that you have never known before.

I have provided you the shoes to run but it is up to you to put them on and break them in. Even shoes that are a perfect fit, as the ones I have gifted you with, need time to be broken in. Listen to me and I will let you know when it is time to walk and when it is time to run.

The Lord God is my strength [my source of courage, my invincible army]; He has made my feet [steady and sure] like hinds' feet and makes me walk [forward with spiritual confidence] on my high places [of challenge and responsibility].
– HABAKKUK 3:19

August

So prepare your minds for action, be completely sober [in spirit—steadfast, self-disciplined, spiritually and morally alert], fix your hope completely on the grace [of God] that is coming to you when Jesus Christ is revealed.

– 1 PETER 1:13

August 1

YOU ARE POWERFUL BECAUSE I AM WITH YOU.
You are not alone. I am your shepherd. Follow me as we cross
over quiet streams. Even if the surroundings are loud and chaotic,
I am the only chance at peace there is, and I will bring it. I will
quiet the storms.

Gird up your loins and follow in my footsteps. Pay close attention,
because sometimes your adversary tries to sweep my footprints
away before you see them. He is the one who draws blinders over
the eyes of my beloved.

I am so proud of you. You are my favorite and I love you. There
is a place in my heart reserved just for you. It is a place with all of
the benefits of my kingdom. They are all for your taking and pure
enjoyment. Do not hesitate; there is no reason to. Nothing that is
of me can bring harm to you.

So prepare your minds for action, be completely sober [in
spirit—steadfast, self-disciplined, spiritually and morally alert],
fix your hope completely on the grace [of God] that is coming to
you when Jesus Christ is revealed.

– 1 PETER 1:13

August 2

I LOVE YOU, MY CHILD. You are so precious to me and so very special. You are the gleam in my eyes. I love you with a love that is everlasting. My hand is always open to you; my arms are always extended. My heart is always inviting you to take your place beside me.

I will open my hands over your head and pour my water over you. Let it refresh and rejuvenate you. Do not stonewall revelation. My love is revelation. It will move you progressively through my heart and will open your eyes. Receive everything that I have for you for. I will never give you more than you can handle.

The Lord appeared to me (Israel) from ages past, saying, "I have loved you with an everlasting love; Therefore with lovingkindness I have drawn you and continued My faithfulness to you.

– JEREMIAH 31:3

For I [fully] satisfy the weary soul, and I replenish every languishing and sorrowful person."

– JEREMIAH 31:25

August 3

CONSIDER A QUIET POOL OF WATER with a gentle fountain; feel the cool breeze caress your skin. Release all of your cares to me. I will give you strength. I will be the support for your footsteps.

Precious child, I love you so much. My love for you is like a never-ending waterfall. You are the shimmer on the surface of the water – bright, sparkling, and beautiful. I have wiped you clean. There are no stains on you. Know and believe it. Stand upright and love mercy. Walk humbly with me; I can show you many great things.

I want you to begin speaking out the things I see when I look at you. There is no reason to listen to that nasty internal dialogue coming from darkness. Speak out the truth of how I feel and think about you. Let those words resonate in your heart.

Guard my soul and rescue me; do not let me be ashamed or disappointed, for I have taken refuge in You. Let integrity and uprightness protect me, for I wait [expectantly] for You

– PSALM 25:20-21

August 4

DO NOT ACTIVELY SEARCH FOR CONTROVERSY to be involved in. Do what you can to honor, respect, and love all those around you. Love them just as I love you. It is those who learn to elevate others who will be elevated.

I love you! Grab that truth and never let go. Let it be a stone that sinks into your heart. You are right where I would like you to be – in my hands. I am proud of you; I will give you even more boldness if you are willing to take it. It is already inside of you. Courage is there as well.

Remember, I do not turn away from weakness. Rather, I am made perfect in weakness. Taste and see that I am good.

But have nothing to do with foolish and ignorant speculations [useless disputes over unedifying, stupid controversies], since you know that they produce strife and give birth to quarrels. The servant of the Lord must not participate in quarrels, but must be kind to everyone [even-tempered, preserving peace, and he must be], skilled in teaching, patient and tolerant when wronged.

– 2 TIMOTHY 2:23-24

August 5

ALL OVER THE WORLD THERE ARE WALLS being raised and torn down inside of my children. Misunderstanding about who I am lets the walls come up; revelation of my love tears them down. I have invited you to come to me with questions that might clear up the confusion. It does not matter what the questions are. Do not be afraid to ask. Wrestle with me through your issues. I promise that I will not get offended.

I love the world. The SON shines on it. Look at the beauty in it and see what I see. I am not blind to the bad, but I look for the good. Enjoy what I have made. Turn your senses to my spirit and search for my fingerprints on the LIFE around you.

For the Lord gives [skillful and godly] wisdom; from His mouth come knowledge and understanding.

– PROVERBS 2:6

August 6

I AM IN YOU; I WILL MOVE THROUGH YOU. I am water and LIFE. I am a cool breeze and the refreshing wind in the desert.

You can see my footsteps in the sand and hear my voice. Follow me, for I am leading the way. But I am in the moment. It is not always about where we are going, but what we can enjoy together right here. Enjoy the things I have placed around you. Laugh and dance with me. Let your cares and concerns float away. I promise that I will not forget about them.

Sometimes a lack of progress toward a goal seems like failure, but it is not. There are times that I need to work behind the scenes. Things are happening even though you cannot see them in the natural. Rest in me and in my love. Be patient; wait for me to finish and we will move forward together.

Cast your burden on the Lord [release it] and He will sustain and uphold you; He will never allow the righteous to be shaken (slip, fall, fail).

– PSALM 55:22

August 7

I AM BREAKING DOWN THE WALLS between you and me. I am crushing them under my foot. I love you. You are a star in my sky that shines so brightly. Recline against me and feel my chest rise and fall.

Let peace be your cloak, for it will keep you warm. It will be your light in the darkness; in the quiet places it will be your voice. Let my peace rule in your heat. It will keep worries on the outside.

Who told you what success looks like? Financial abundance, high positions, and material possessions do not equal success in my kingdom. You are a success because of who you are in me, not because you have met the world's definition. My love declares you to be a success.

You have put joy in my heart, more than [others know] when their wheat and new wine have yielded abundantly. In peace [and with a tranquil heart] I will both lie down and sleep, for You alone, O Lord, make me dwell in safety and confident trust.

– PSALM 4:7-8

August 8

THERE IS NO GREATER LOVER THAN ME. There is no greater lover than one who lays down his life. I am the fullness of love and joy. The music of your heart is sweet; I could sway to its beat forever. Notice the twinkle in my eye and understand that you are the cause. My smile is for you. Living in this revelation will chase the clouds from your spirit.

The bread of LIFE causes maturation. My table is always open. Sit down, rest, and feast on my bread even as your enemies gather. I am pouring my spirit out into your midst. Watch as the floods rise and carry LIFE to the dry lands. The creaks and groans are hearts turning to me and away from the empty pursuit of the world.

No one has greater love [nor stronger commitment] than to lay down his own life for his friends.

– JOHN 15:13

August 9

I AM THRIVING AND STRONG WITHIN YOU and am reaching out to those around you. I am working even when you are not, and moving even when you do not realize it. It is a beautiful thing when you reflect my love and it does not seem unusual to you. Be encouraged and of good cheer, for I am with you.

Take my strength when you need it. I will never hold it out of your reach. In the same way, you should freely give to others what I have given to you. I will give the qualities of my heart to whoever asks. My desire is that you look more like me every day. Will you let me fashion you into my image?

O give thanks to the Lord, call upon His name; make known His deeds among the people. Sing to Him, sing praises to Him; speak of all His wonderful acts and devoutly praise them.

– PSALM 105:1-2

August 10

I AM ARRANGING A COUPLE of paths for yoU. When many go out at the same time it can look like a tangled mess. But I see from above, and I am weaving them together in ways you cannot recognize right now. Just trust in me and in how much I love you. Keep walking straight and I will conform your feet to the twists and bends in the road. You are not walking some arbitrary, meaningless path. It is leading somewhere good.

Relax in my love for you. Just know that nearly every opportunity to step out will be uncomfortable. I am asking you to do it anyway. You have the tools to overcome any objections your adversary might shout. Use those tools.

Blessed [happy, spiritually prosperous, favored by God] is the man who is steadfast under trial and perseveres when tempted; for when he has passed the test and been approved, he will receive the [victor's] crown of life which the Lord has promised to those who love Him.

– JAMES 1:12

August 11

THE MORE YOU COME TO KNOW ME the more you are transformed into a weapon that is always advancing against the darkness. Each step you take is an offensive attack against the enemy. It is when you take a step and the enemy does *not* notice, that there is a problem. Your adversary should always take note of what you are doing.

Be a living sacrifice; be dedicated to me and show the world what my love looks like. You can do this. It is not you who live, but I who live in you. Stop trying to be perfect and just be!

For our struggle is not against flesh and blood [contending only with physical opponents], but against the rulers, against the powers, against the world forces of this [present] darkness, against the spiritual forces of wickedness in the heavenly (supernatural) places.

– EPHESIANS 6:12

August 12

YOU ARE A LABOR OF MY LOVE. It gives me joy to work with you and in you to bring forth everything I have planned for you.

It is my breath that gives LIFE to the things lying dormant inside of my children. My words are like water. My body is the shade to keep you from being scorched.

I love you so much. Look at me and understand who I am. Do not look to your own understanding, but let me change and transform your thinking into my own thoughts and processes.

For we are His workmanship [His own master work, a work of art], created in Christ Jesus [reborn from above—spiritually transformed, renewed, ready to be used] for good works, which God prepared [for us] beforehand [taking paths which He set], so that we would walk in them [living the good life which He prearranged and made ready for us].

– EPHESIANS 2:10

August 13

JUST LET GO AND FALL INTO ME. I will catch you. You are free and you are loved. I am digging up the treasure being formed in your heart. The world needs to see it. Once they do they will want it for themselves. The things I have taught you and the ways you have grown need to be available for others. They will come to you for it. Honor and lift them up. It makes my heart glad to watch you be an open vessel for me to work through.

Give thanks; let gratitude be a song of your heart. You shall have the abundance I have in store for you. Some blessings are like savings bonds. You need to mature to a certain point before I can release them to you.

You have because I have given. I am the source of LIFE. Remember that. If you wander to other sources, you will find the well dry. Stay deeply rooted in me.

But we have this precious treasure [the good news about salvation] in [unworthy] earthen vessels [of human frailty], so that the grandeur and surpassing greatness of the power will be [shown to be] from God [His sufficiency] and not from ourselves.
– 2 CORINTHIANS 4:7

August 14

JUST REST IN ME. Lay down your agenda and let me just love on you. Commit to being with me here in this moment. I am here with you. Set your eyes on the things above for they are the things that bring LIFE. Death comes from below and LIFE comes from above.

I love you; you are so precious to me. Seek to understand who I am and then help others to do the same. I am pleased with you; you make me smile. I am outfitting you with the tools and equipment you will need for the journey ahead. You are not unprepared.

I want you to be who I created you to be. You are so wonderful; it would be a shame to deprive the world of everything you have to offer.

Return to your rest, O my soul, for the Lord has dealt bountifully with you.

– PSALM 116:7

August 15

LET US GET DEEPER INTO WHAT IS GOING ON – underneath some of the external circumstances and events of life. Travel farther with me into your heart and into the message I have given you to walk in. I will bring even more understanding to you. Confusion is not something that comes from me. I will bring clarity to your mind. You shall know the plans I have for you and how to accomplish them. You have hope and you have a future.

Do not despise the pace I have you on. "The grass is always greener" is a specialty used by your adversary. I would not have you in a place where you could not be content. You can be content because of the security my love provides.

I know how to get along and live humbly [in difficult times], and I also know how to enjoy abundance and live in prosperity. In any and every circumstance I have learned the secret [of facing life], whether well-fed or going hungry, whether having an abundance or being in need. I can do all things [which He has called me to do] through Him who strengthens and empowers me [to fulfill His purpose—I am self-sufficient in Christ's sufficiency; I am ready for anything and equal to anything through Him who infuses me with inner strength and confident peace.]

– PHILIPPIANS 4:12-13

August 16

JUST BREATHE. IT IS GOING TO BE OKAY. Trust me and know that I have a way.

Do not allow money to be your motivation. You will never be able to have peace if money is what drives you. I know what you need and I have a plan. Listen and be sensitive to my leading, and you will find my river overflowing with abundance.

I hear the sound of your heart. Let it beat for me. Let it beat for love and peace. There is no strife in a heart that beats for me because it is at rest. I love you so much. I adore you. Rest in, and trust, that love.

The Lord will open for you His good treasure house, the heavens, to give rain to your land in its season and to bless all the work of your hand; and you will lend to many nations, but you will not borrow.

– DEUTERONOMY 28:12

August 17

I AM YOUR PERFECT DADDY AND I LOVE YOU. I have clothed you in splendor. Look how bright you shine! I delight in you. Walk beside me and enjoy life. I am power; I am LIFE; I am victory.

Be patient, and wait for me to plug in the stops along your path. If you try and plug them in yourself, you are going to end up with a big mess. I am a God of order and I am the conductor of a great symphony. I am the one who guides those playing off-key back into unity. Do not strive; simply rest in me.

For God [who is the source of their prophesying] is not a God of confusion and disorder but of peace and order.

– 1 CORINTHIANS 14:33

August 18

BE WARY OF THE WORD *NEED*. All you *need* is my love. Find your worth and value in me and let them remain fastened to my heart. No matter what happens, you are so valuable and deeply loved beyond measure. I cannot even measure my love for you because it has no end. There is not a container big enough for it.

What box or container is big enough for me? When you try to place me in a box, it is really you who gets trapped in it. It becomes a prison for you, not for me. I have come so that you can be free, not locked in chains.

I am the Lord, I have called You (the Messiah) in righteousness [for a righteous purpose], I will also take You by the hand and keep watch over You, and I will appoint You as a covenant to the people [Israel], as a light to the nations (Gentiles), to open the eyes of the blind, to bring out prisoners from the dungeon and those who sit in darkness from the prison.

– ISAIAH 42:6-7

August 19

THE CLOUDS PART BECAUSE MY RADIANCE shines through and breaks the grey. Walk in my valley and stop to admire all that is in it. LIFE flourishes because I am here. Everything grows because there is no death. There is nothing but abundance here in my valley.

This is how it can be in your life. Death does not need to be a part of your life because you can walk in LIFE. You can walk in love and you can be a living invitation for others to do the same. When you live this way, you are reflecting me and it is noticed. Every smile or friendly hello is an extension of my kingdom. It is the silence that separates.

Open up to me. I am here for you. What do you want to talk about?

He will swallow up death [and abolish it] for all time. And the Lord God will wipe away tears from all faces, and He will take away the disgrace of His people from all the earth; for the Lord has spoken.

– ISAIAH 25:8

August 20

CONSIDER A LINE OF WELLS reaching deep into the earth. The wells are filled with my love and joy. Buckets constantly come to draw the water. The wells will never run dry; I have so much to give. If my love does not go forward, it is not a reflection on me but on those who are supposed to be carrying it.

Look for the good things – the beneficial things. Whatever is lovely and of a good report is a reflection of me. Darkness, in any form, comes from your adversary. He is already defeated. I want you to live in dominion over him. I have given you all the power and authority you need to do so. Take the tools I have given you and subdue the earth.

And God blessed them [granting them certain authority] and said to them, "Be fruitful, multiply, and fill the earth, and subjugate it [putting it under your power]; and rule over (dominate) the fish of the sea, the birds of the air, and every living thing that moves upon the earth.

– GENESIS 1:28

August 21

REST WITH ME. YOU ARE OKAY. I am a refreshing wind and I want you to let me blow through you. Let's take things one step at a time. Your worth and identity are not tied to the things you accomplish. They are tied to me and what I have accomplished in you.

I love you so much. You are a pleasure to me. I am holding out my hand to you and I want to you take it. The storms will come. There will be a few showers and then the thunder; a few quivers and then the quake. Be ready and stand firm. Listen to me and I will guide you through the turns. You will not be undone.

Beware of the wisdom the world has to offer. Many have taken it in times of need and found themselves drowning. I will lead you out of troubled waters, not further into them.

For the wisdom of this world is foolishness (absurdity, stupidity) before God; for it is written [in Scripture], "[He is] The one who catches the wise and clever in their craftiness;" and again, "The Lord knows the thoughts of the [humanly] wise, that they are useless."

– 1 CORINTHIANS 3:19-20

August 22

THERE IS A DAM IN FRONT OF YOU RIGHT NOW, and I am managing what gets through. I will not give you more than you can handle. As we move forward, I will open the passage more and more and you will notice the increase. Do not despise my pace for there is great purpose in it. Stay with me and stay steady.

Do not compare the speed of your journey with the speed of others. I dance differently with different people and I equip my children in unique ways. Dance with me and let me lead.

Wait for and confidently expect the Lord; be strong and let your heart take courage; yes, wait for and confidently expect the Lord.

– PSALM 27:14

August 23

CONSIDER A TWIG THAT SNAPS INTO TWO PIECES. Now consider my children. There are some who will break right away because they have allowed themselves to become malnourished. As a result, they are dry and brittle.

But there are others who will bend instead of breaking. Connective tissue will stretch but it will all hold together no matter the strain. These are those who are properly nourished because I am with them and infused into them. My spirit in them is alive and active, and I have made them strong. They shall not break. The enemy shall not advance his will over them.

Do not forget who I am in you. This is the foundation of victory – that you are loved and that I am in you.

They will fight against you, but they will not [ultimately] prevail over you, for I am with you [always] to protect you and deliver you," says the Lord.

– JEREMIAH 1:19

August 24

MY LOVE GUSHES LIKE A GEYSER. Sometimes it is more forceful and sometimes it is gentler. But every time it is overwhelming. There is no greater joy than to know just how much I love you.

My love surrounds you like water that you can breathe, and it is the sweetest breath you will ever take. When you breathe it in, it reaches every cell and brings you out of your slumber. Take one breath at a time. Do not rush. I will fill you; I promise.

There is a very real tie between your heart and mine. Acknowledge me in all you do and you will experience increase in every area of your life. There is no dam big enough to hold back the abundance I have in store for you.

What do you want from me? How do you want to experience me?

Bless and affectionately praise the Lord, O my soul, and all that is [deep] within me, bless His holy name. Bless and affectionately praise the Lord, O my soul, and do not forget any of His benefits.

– PSALM 103:1-2

August 25

I LOVE YOU; YOU MAKE ME SO HAPPY. You make me laugh, and I could just watch you all day long. I really do watch you all day long.

I know that there can be some hesitation in you when I talk like that. There are times that I can feel the check in your gut. Sometimes you still see yourself as unworthy of those words. But that is not the truth. It is a lie and I want you to get rid of it. You have my joy down deep in your heart. Do not let anyone or anything tell you different.

Do not let the lies from the enemy take up residence in your heart. Seek me for the truth and make the choice to believe my words.

O Lord, you have searched me [thoroughly] and have known me. You know when I sit down and when I rise up [my entire life, everything I do]; You understand my thought from afar. You scrutinize my path and my lying down, and You are intimately acquainted with all my ways.

– PSALM 139:1-3

August 26

I AM REDEFINING THINGS IN YOUR HEART. At times this can be uncomfortable. I never promised that the journey with me would always be a comfortable one. There are things along the way that can make it difficult. The things that make it difficult are not always external factors. Many times they come from within as minds are renewed into the truth I reveal.

I am revealing truth on a large scale. Some are not ready for it and will lag behind. To those who can grasp it, it will be revelation that sets them free in ways they have always longed for but could not seem to achieve.

I am the light that has come into the darkness, but the world did not recognize the light. The shade is retreating and I am revealing my fullness in this age, in this hour. You must be willing to look in order to see it unfold. I promise that the reward you shall receive is worth the momentary discomfort.

[We pray that you may be] strengthened and invigorated with all power, according to His glorious might, to attain every kind of endurance and patience with joy; giving thanks to the Father, who has qualified us to share in the inheritance of the saints (God's people) in the Light.

– COLOSSIANS 1:11-12

❧ *August 27* ❧

CONSIDER FLAKES OF SNOW gently falling through the air. They dance and float as they make their way to the ground. Sometimes they land and stick. Other times they melt right away.

The ground must be ready to receive my love. The hot fire of shame, guilt, and condemnation often melts the flakes of my love and purity, and must be extinguished in order for my love to stick.

I do not want you to punish yourself at all. There is a difference between feeling bad and locking handcuffs around your wrists until you feel like it has been long enough. I did not come so that you could live in prison. I came to bring you freedom and LIFE. Take off the locks!

Do not fear, for you will not be put to shame, and do not feel humiliated or ashamed, for you will not be disgraced. For you will forget the shame of your youth, and you will no longer remember the disgrace of your widowhood.

– ISAIAH 54:4

August 28

THE SUN RISES AND THE SON HAS RISEN. Both shine light over the earth, but only one is eternal. Be careful how much you invest into the temporary things of this world, for the old is passing away and the new is coming with my mighty wind. Invest yourself into my kingdom, for that is the only thing that will remain.

I love you so much. Walk in my footsteps today. Take my hand and let me lead you. We will walk together. Pass through my waterfalls, for times of spiritual refreshing are coming to you. This is one of those times. Stand under the fountain of my love. Let it caress you and hold you close.

The grass withers, the flower fades, but the word of our God stands forever.

– ISAIAH 40:8

August 29

SEEK AND YOU SHALL FIND. Knock and the door will be open to you. Let the song of your heart be the melody of mine.

You will soar with me and I will show you things up close that were previously far away. You shall not become part of the status quo; rather you will stand strong against it. Let my words pour from your mouth and change the direction of the flow. You will see the bigger picture, but you will also see how to get there. This is the road I have you on.

Some will pass you unaffected by your stance, but some will notice. They will stop and stand with you. You will start to see the direction of the current change before your eyes. It is renewal. It is hearts and minds being transformed into my image.

I am giving you a new commandment, that you love one another. Just as I have loved you, so you too are to love one another. By this everyone will know that you are My disciples, if you have love and unselfish concern for one another.

– JOHN 13:34-35

JESSE AND KARA BIRKEY

August 30

I LOVE YOU SO MUCH. Let my love be the message of your heart and life. Be on your guard. The enemy is going to try and center your LIFE around other things – things that are temporary and already passing away.

Let the change my love brings be your motivation instead of the rewards that the world has to offer. The *eternal* rewards come from me. Believe that I am good and that I will reward those who earnestly seek me. I will reward you in the open for the quiet choices you make to stay in my loving embrace.

The message is my love. There is no other foundation on which LIFE can stand. On what foundation are you standing?

So everyone who hears these words of Mine and acts on them, will be like a wise man [a far-sighted, practical, and sensible man] who built his house on the rock. And the rain fell, and the floods and torrents came, and the winds blew and slammed against that house; yet it did not fall, because it had been founded on the rock.

– MATTHEW 7:24-25

August 31

YOU ARE LOVED; YOU ARE MY CHILD. My love has defined you; it tells you who you are.

Consider battery posts that have corrosion built up around them. The connection cannot get through as well as it should, and the system keeps shorting out. I want to clean the connection between us so that you can hear me clearly. I will reveal to you the things that cause the build-up.

The cares of this world have a tendency to draw your eyes off of me. They bring in stress, worry, and dread, causing interference between us. Keep your eyes and ears open to what I am doing and saying. I have placed an overflowing bowl of peace over your head; let my peace consume you.

For you [who are born-again have been reborn from above—spiritually transformed, renewed, sanctified and] are all children of God [set apart for His purpose with full rights and privileges] through faith in Christ Jesus.

– GALATIANS 3:26

September

Therefore encourage and comfort one another and build up one another, just as you are doing.

— 1 THESSALONIANS 5:11

September 1

THERE ARE STILL SOME THINGS, other than me, that you believe can give you LIFE, but they cannot give you what you need. LIFE is in me and nothing else can be the source for you. It is not wrong to have things, but your adversary will use them to try to define you. Do not let that happen. I will give you the strength you need to resist the temptation to reach out for false comforts. Reach for my love instead, and be filled. When you are getting all of your LIFE from me, there is no room for anything else in the foundation of your identity.

Reflect me in all you do. Learn how to serve; be an encouraging voice; love above all else. Lift up and never tear down.

Therefore encourage and comfort one another and build up one another, just as you are doing.

– 1 THESSALONIANS 5:11

September 2

I WILL PROVIDE FOR YOU. There is no question about that on my end. Let there be no doubt on yours. It shall be done. This is a promise, so grab and hold onto it.

Do not let your heart be troubled. I know the answer for what you are facing. Trust my wisdom and release it to me. Command the voice of fear to be silent. Close your ears to every voice but mine. I will lead you to the Promised Land that I have prepared for you. Follow my footsteps. I will make them easy to find, but you must be looking for them.

Let your disappointment sink like the moon, and your hope, joy, and trust in me rise like the sun. You are still in the center of my palm. I love you so much. Let my love cover you like a warm blanket.

You have a strong arm; mighty is Your hand, Your right hand is exalted. Righteousness and justice are the foundation of Your throne; lovingkindness and truth go before You. Blessed and happy are the people who know the joyful sound [of the trumpet's blast]! they walk, O Lord, in the light and favor of Your countenance!

– PSALM 89:13-15

September 3

DO NOT BE DISMAYED, FOR I AM YOUR GOD. I will lift you from the gritty sand and plant you in an oasis. My love is liquid to your lips; it will energize your soul, spirit, and body.

I love our time together. It lets me reset your heart for the day, like a clockmaker resets a clock that is not ticking quite right. This is the time that your eyes can find me. Let your heart settle into mine. The things I have in store for you sparkle like diamonds.

I have you on a sifter; there is much gold that is breaking loose. You are becoming more and more like me. The day is coming that I will complete the work I started in you and gold will be all that is left. But even now your beauty is matchless.

O magnify the Lord with me, and let us lift up His name together. I sought the Lord [on the authority of His word], and He answered me, and delivered me from all my fears. They looked to Him and were radiant; their faces will never blush in shame or confusion.

– PSALM 34:3-5

September 4

I CHERISH YOU. You are highly favored and adored. I want you to believe it. You have decided to walk in my ways and for that you have been rewarded.

I will take you deeper inside of my heart. There is so much more for you that I have not revealed yet. I need to peel back the layers slowly. Trust my pace in all things. I do not hold back because I love you less; I hold back because I do not want to ruin you.

Speak my name and things will change around you. I have outfitted you to do the work I have called you to do, and I am going to give you even more tools to use.

Let Your work [the signs of Your power] be revealed to Your servants and Your [glorious] majesty to their children. And let the [gracious] favor of the Lord our God be on us; confirm for us the work of our hands—yes, confirm the work of our hands.

– PSALM 90:16-17

September 5

I AM BEGINNING TO UNLOCK NEW GIFTS inside of you. Be ready to receive them.

The gifts I give you are intended to be a blessing to you and to those around you. Receive my blessings as they come, but do not be dependent upon the blessings. Be dependent upon me.

Learning to just be in my presence is the greatest gift. As you grow in this, everything else will thrive as well. Everything fruitful in your life will be birthed during this time.

Just as each one of you has received a special gift [a spiritual talent, an ability graciously given by God], employ it in serving one another as [is appropriate for] good stewards of God's multi-faceted grace [faithfully using the diverse, varied gifts and abilities granted to Christians by God's unmerited favor].

– 1 PETER 4:10

September 6

CONSIDER A SWING IN A QUIET PARK. Take a seat on the swing and let me push you. Feel the wind through your hair as your concerns fall away. All the cares of the world shall pass away in my presence. The peace that emanates from me untangles the problems of the world as if they were never tangled at all. Problems align themselves before me.

Do not give shame, guilt, and condemnation access into your heart. Look for ways throughout the day in which you were successful in loving instead of focusing on the times you were not.

I am opening you up to new revelations, and to some old ones that will feel new. I am going to draw back the curtain of revelation for you. You will see me in new ways. Are you ready for that?

Your way, O God, is holy [far from sin and guilt]. What god is great like our God? You are the [awesome] God who works [powerful] wonders; You have demonstrated Your power among the people.

– PSALM 77:13-14

September 7

WHEN YOU OPEN YOUR MOUTH TO PRAY, a river of LIFE comes out and floods everything around you.

I cannot wait to walk through this day with you. I want to just be with you. This is how I look at every day. It is my joy and pleasure to walk with you and show you the work of my hands. Listen to me as I share my heart. Let my soft voice quiet your objections. Yes, I love you that much. Yes, I adore you that much.

Let your heart be overrun by my goodness. My goodness is like honey – sweet with healing properties. I am medicine for every part of your body. I am the healer and I make all things new. Let the old pass away and focus on what is before you. The past is done. It cannot be changed. Let's move on – pressing upward and onward to the things I have laid out for you.

Will you follow me?

I love the Lord, because He hears [and continues to hear] my voice and my supplications (my pleas, my cries, my specific needs). Because He has inclined His ear to me, therefore I will call on Him as long as I live.

– PSALM 116:1-2

September 8

IT IS MY INTENTION to continually lift you higher. There will be periods of time that the progress will be horizontal, but the movement will never be backwards or downwards. I am the lifter of your head and your feet.

Be deeply planted in me; let your roots reach into my heart. There is a plentiful harvest ahead of you and we are going into the field. Many will be touched; many will come to know me. Clap your hands and be happy. Let my joy register on your face.

Stress comes when you take your eyes off of mine, so fix them on me. I am not bound by the natural limitations of this world. I operate in the supernatural, which is how I will provide for you. I will supply all of your needs according to my riches in glory!

And my God will liberally supply (fill until full) your every need according to His riches in glory in Christ Jesus.
– PHILIPPIANS 4:19

September 9

MY LOVE IS LIKE AN ACTIVE VOLCANO, constantly erupting, covering, and consuming all within its reach.

You are a plant that I am growing into a beautiful tree. I am constantly tending to you and watching over you. Point your petals at me in the same way sunflowers face the sun. Focus on me and we will grow together. I promise that your knowledge of me will increase because I really want to share myself with you. I want to share my heart, my thoughts, my desires, my power, authority, and miracles.

Come and share in my LIFE. We are workers in the field removing the layers of dead brush in order to reach the rich soil underneath. Work with me to make dry, barren lands beautiful.

O Lord, truly I am Your servant; I am Your servant, the son of Your handmaid; You have unfastened my chains. I will offer to You the sacrifice of thanksgiving, and will call on the name of the Lord.

– PSALM 116:16-17

September 10

ALWAYS KEEP A WATCH over your mouth, my beloved. Your words hold so much more power than you are aware of. In your words are LIFE and death.

It only takes a second with an unrestrained tongue to cause a world of pain and damage. Pause before speaking, and while you pause, ask for wisdom. I will give you the words to speak and reveal to you when it is time to simply be silent. Much silence is required for humility.

Remember, my kingdom is not the same as the kingdom of the world. Having adequate knowledge for a situation does not necessarily give you the right to share. Use your words as a vessel to share my love with the world.

Set a guard, O Lord, over my mouth; keep watch over the door of my lips [to keep me from speaking thoughtlessly].

– PSALM 141:3

He who has knowledge restrains and is careful with his words, and a man of understanding and wisdom has a cool spirit (self-control, an even temper).

– PROVERBS 17:27

September 11

I AM DOING A NEW THING IN YOUR LIFE. Let your spirit and heart rest in my hands. Like a child who lies down in the crib at night, let your mind rest in me. There is nothing you can think about that I have not already considered. I know all and see all. Nothing is hidden from me, not even answers to the problems that seem larger than the tallest mountains.

Let me remind you never to look down on anyone. You have met some who have been carrying profound revelation that was not apparent on the exterior. The outside might seem trodden and worn out, but their hearts are more alive than most. Look with eyes of love, not judgment.

And He who sits on the throne said, "Behold, I am making all things new." Also He said, "Write, for these words are faithful and true [they are accurate, incorruptible, and trustworthy]."

– REVELATION 21:5

September 12

THE WORK OF YOUR HANDS will produce sweet fruit and a bountiful harvest. I am the great gardener, and I have invited you into the field to work with me. Look out for the thieves. They sneak in and try to snatch the harvest. In their hands, the ripe fruit rots and turns into mush.

Stay close to me. Do not wander out on your own. The lie of independence seduces many into a false sense of security. Many think that they are on solid ground when they are actually hovering in the air with nothing beneath their feet.

When you are walking with me, the road will always meet your feet. There is always a solid foundation in me. You cannot fall because you never leave the ground. Stay with me. Seek my wisdom in all you do. I will let you know when to move.

The thief comes only in order to steal and kill and destroy. I came that they may have and enjoy life, and have it in abundance [to the full, till it overflows].

– JOHN 10:10

❧[*September 13*]❧

LET ME TELL YOU ABOUT MY DAUGHTERS – they are so precious to me. They always have been. I love the giggles and prancing that comes with the freedom of a little girl; they perfectly manifest my heart in so many ways.

Look at me, child. Look at my face. It is calm and steady. There is no worry in my eyes; no flash of apprehension breaks my smile. This is how I am even in the midst of storms. I know at any time I can say, "Peace be still," and it will be still. You have the same ability.

There are people around you who can help you walk the path I have for you. Do not ignore them. Do not despise the people who can help you. Let them help you with the gifts and abilities I have given them. Take great courage and reach out when you need a shoulder to lean on.

Without consultation and wise advice, plans are frustrated, but with many counselors they are established and succeed.

– PROVERBS 15:22

September 14

I WANT TO TELL YOU A FEW THINGS while I wrap my arms around you. I love you. You are my joy, yes, my joy. I am proud of you and I delight in you. All of the good things I have done and placed in you shine brightly. Those around you take notice.

If you could remember me as often as you take a breath, you would be doing great. But that is not to say you are not doing great already. There is grace for your walk. I do not wait until my kids think about me to act. I am always moving and working on behalf of those who love me and live for me. But I can do so much more when I am invited to be a part of every moment. Will you invite me into every moment with you?

I will [solemnly] remember the deeds of the Lord; yes, I will [wholeheartedly] remember Your wonders of old. I will meditate on all Your works and thoughtfully consider all Your [great and wondrous] deeds.

– PSALM 77:11-12

September 15

DANCE, CHILD, DANCE! Dancing represents complete freedom in me. The worries of this world will melt away when you dance.

Let the praises of your heart be the music of your LIFE. Let the praises of my name forever be on your lips, for they will bring LIFE to your circumstances.

When the enemy throws trials and temptations your way, come in the opposite spirit and he will flee! Light extinguishes darkness in every situation.

Praise Him with tambourine and dancing; Praise Him with stringed instruments and flute.

— PSALM 150:4

So submit to [the authority of] God. Resist the devil [stand firm against him] and he will flee from you.

— JAMES 4:7

September 16

ANY TIME YOU CAN TAKE TO JUST GET QUIET and be with me is going to renew your heart and refresh your peace. I will meet you anywhere, anytime. I will pursue you across great distances – across anything that might stand between us.

I am excited for you to share with others the things I have taught you. I am going to really bless people through your willingness to be a reflection of me. I will fill your heart with courage and love so that you can show me to the world. The day is spread before you like an open book; let's write in it together.

Let me hear Your loving kindness in the morning, for I trust in You. Teach me the way in which I should walk, for I lift up my soul to You.

– PSALM 143:8

September 17

I HAVE PREPARED YOU FOR THIS DAY like a delicious cake – firm yet soft, warm and ready for what goes on top. I will layer you with frosting and berries. Let those around you have a slice of you today. It will be sweet on their tongues and in their bellies. You are a delight to me, and you will be a delight to those around you.

You make me smile. Did you know that? I smile at you all the time. I wish you would see that more. I know how your heart is filled each time you remember my smile. Be a blessing to those around you today. Let goodness and light, mercy and grace, flow from your heart.

Keep all darkness far from you. You will not be tempted beyond what you can bear. It cannot overcome you. You must not let it take you. Make the choice to stand strong in my steadfast love and I will defeat the foes before you.

Therefore, my beloved, run [keep far, far away] from [any sort of] idolatry [and that includes loving anything more than God, or participating in anything that leads to sin and enslaves the soul].

– 1 CORINTHIANS 10:14

September 18

NOTHING SHALL HINDER OR KEEP YOU from walking forward on the path I have marked out for you. Nothing, that is, but you. Do not let fear grip your heart and keep you stuck in the mud. Continue to take steps forward, because each step, no matter how small, will take you into greater revelation. Each step brings something new.

I love you so much. I have come for you and I am leading you. The darkness gathers like storm clouds, but I have overcome. My light will always shine through because it cannot be smothered. I love you so much; I am *for* you. All that I have, I give to you.

For God did not give us a spirit of timidity or cowardice or fear, but [He has given us a spirit] of power and of love and of sound judgment and personal discipline [abilities that result in a calm, well-balanced mind and self-control].

– 2 TIMOTHY 1:7

September 19

GAZE INTO MY EYES AND SEE the wonder that is there. That wonder is what I am inviting you into; it is where I am trying to lead you. Be strong and courageous. Trust me in the process and trust the pace. Keep your ears open to my voice. Practice listening to me so that you can separate my voice from the rest.

I am here with you even when you cannot see or feel me. I never leave your side; we walk hand in hand. My glory shines beyond what you can see and lights the way. It is going to be okay. A treasure trove of jewels lies ahead of you. You are walking in the abundant LIFE I came to bring. I will bless the work of your hands.

You, in Your great mercy and compassion, did not abandon them in the wilderness; the pillar of the cloud did not leave them by day, to lead them in the way, nor the pillar of fire by night, to light for them the way they should go.

– NEHEMIAH 9:19

September 20

HOPE COMES FROM KNOWING ME. Outside of me there is no hope. Life is fleeting but I am eternal. My hope breathes LIFE into dry bones.

This world has nothing of true value to offer on its own. My kingdom has everything to offer. When your hope fades, take heart in knowing that I have a bottomless well to replenish your thirsty soul. Come to me and drink. One sip will not do. Drink continuously, every second if you need to. My well will never run dry and is always available to you.

Blessed [gratefully praised and adored] be the God and Father of our Lord Jesus Christ, who according to His abundant and boundless mercy has caused us to be born again [that is, to be reborn from above—spiritually transformed, renewed, and set apart for His purpose] to an ever-living hope and confident assurance through the resurrection of Jesus Christ from the dead, [born anew] into an inheritance which is imperishable [beyond the reach of change] and undefiled and unfading, reserved in heaven for you.

– 1 PETER 1:3-4

Hope deferred makes the heart sick, but when desire is fulfilled, it is a tree of life.

– PROVERBS 13:12

September 21

I LOVE THE WORLD. There are so many more things that make me smile than make me frown. I am proud of you. The things you are doing are making a difference. You are making a tremendous impact on the world around you.

Consider ripples spreading out across the surface of water. Your actions reach much further than you think. I know it is hard to walk this way, but trust me. Things are happening. Remember what I have spoken to you and trust me. I will not let my words return void.

But have peace and remember what I have asked of you. Do justly, love mercy, and walk with me. Are you doing those things?

For God so [greatly] loved and dearly prized the world, that He [even] gave His [One and] only begotten Son, so that whoever believes and trusts in Him [as Savior] shall not perish, but have eternal life.

– JOHN 3:16

September 22

TREAT THE HEARTS OF THOSE AROUND YOU like precious jewels. Polish them and wrap them up in protection. Do not allow them to fall to the ground, or do anything that might leave them chipped, stained, or cloudy. You will not be able to relate to everyone in the same way. Adapt as necessary. Love is constant, but the way you relate to different people changes – it is dynamic.

Do not elevate yourself above those who are younger than you. Self-sacrificial love does not waver based on age. Love will look different in different situations, but in every case, the other person is highly valued and honored.

Let self-sacrificial love be the foundation of every relationship you have. How do you relate to those around you?

Love is to be sincere and active [the real thing—without guile and hypocrisy]. Hate what is evil [detest all ungodliness, do not tolerate wickedness]; hold on tightly to what is good. Be devoted to one another with [authentic] brotherly affection [as members of one family], give preference to one another in honor
– ROMANS 12:9-10

September 23

HEY, THE RAIN IS CLEARING. The sun is going to shine, and it is going to be a great day. But even when the clouds cover the sky, my love is shining on you. You do not need to let external circumstances determine your mood or how you feel. You are always connected to me. You are always connected to my heart. That means you are always connected to love and joy. Do not wander off because of gathering clouds.

I know it can be hard not to be influenced by your surroundings. Just remember that I am always in your surroundings. Choose to be influenced by me. Let all of the noise fade away and focus on my voice – my presence.

And behold, the glory and brilliance of the God of Israel was coming from the way of the east; and His voice was like the sound of many waters, and the earth shone with His glory.

– EZEKIEL 43:2

❦ *September 24* ❧

I WILL GIVE YOU MORE. You are not stuck on a ledge; you are moving forward. Take a moment and look around. You are out here in the open air and I am the one holding you up. I am continually pouring myself into you – reaching further down into who you are. I am the revelation and the LIFE. Come to me and you will know me. I will not hide myself from you.

The birds of the air fly without thought about how they are staying up. So shall you be free from concern as to how you will remain on the road. You do not have to worry because I am guiding your feet. The way ahead is safe. You will give no thought to those who lie in wait for your ruin because I have already gone before you to clear the way.

You who fear the Lord [with awe-inspired reverence], praise Him! All you descendants of Jacob, honor Him. Fear Him [with submissive wonder], all you descendants of Israel. For He has not despised nor detested the suffering of the afflicted; nor has He hidden His face from him; but when he cried to Him for help, He listened.

– PSALM 22:23-24

September 25

I TAKE GREAT DELIGHT IN SPENDING time with you. It does not always have to be so serious. Picture yourself with me in a large, lush field full of wild flowers. I love to walk and talk with you while we admire the beauty surrounding us. Let loose and skip, sing, and dance with me. Sit under the shade of a tree and share your day with me. In my presence is fullness of joy.

When the world makes you weary, I will restore your strength. Recognition of my presence only takes a second. Take a breath and breathe me in. My Spirit will refresh you in a supernatural way.

May the God of hope fill you with all joy and peace in believing [through the experience of your faith] that by the power of the Holy Spirit you will abound in hope and overflow with confidence in His promises.

– ROMANS 15:13

September 26

IF YOU LOOK TO ME IN YOUR SUFFERING, you will get to see me in ways you might not have before. If you can lift your head, I will lift the rest. That is why heaviness wants to keep you down and blinded. If you can see me, you can overcome.

I am doing a new thing in your life and in your heart. Do not resist the process because I am bringing you into something greater than you had before. I would not start a work in you that I was not going to finish, and I would not start it if it were not going to be good for you.

I will bring you the resources you need to the do the work I have called you to do. Cast all of your cares on me. I would not call you to begin something that you could not finish. Look to me for direction. I know the desires of your heart. Do not think for a moment that they are not important to me. Let my love cover you.

Even to your old age I am He, and even to your advanced old age I will carry you! I have made you, and I will carry you; be assured I will carry you and I will save you.

– ISAIAH 46:4

September 27

YOU ARE SO SPECIAL TO ME. Rest in the knowledge that I am working for you to provide everything you need for your enjoyment. Do not run ahead and force anything.

I am a refreshing spring and I am pouring over you right now. Let me saturate you as you move through the day. I am the fountain of living water and I will never dry up. I will refresh and renew you.

Do not be dismayed at what you might see standing in front of you. Command the mountains to move in my name. Stare down the enemy and command your foes to move out of your way. Do not allow them to overtake you for they come against you like a wave. You shall not be overcome. I am with you. With a word they are shaken. With a shout they crumble. I am your strength and shield. Stay with me and you will not be harmed – you will be exalted. I will take what the enemy designed for evil and use it for your good.

O [reverently] fear the Lord, you His saints (believers, holy ones); for to those who fear Him there is no want. The young lions lack [food] and grow hungry, but they who seek the Lord will not lack any good thing.

– PSALM 34:9-10

September 28

I LOVE YOU, AND I AM HERE. I am the dew on the ground – fresh and new. My presence makes the whole world glisten. Let your heart be full of thanksgiving.

I have created in you a clean heart. It is new and full, bursting with the love that comes from my throne. Keep your eyes on me and you will not fall into the holes and traps that seek to entangle you. Walk on the highway of holiness. Do not let the things of the world pull you down into the tangled vines.

Actively pursue peace, love, honor, and respect. Let your mind and heart rest on the things that come from above – the things that come from my heart.

Now may God give you of the dew of heaven [to water your land], and of the fatness (fertility) of the earth, and an abundance of grain and new wine.

– GENESIS 27:28

September 29

IF YOU GIVE YOUR HEART TO ME, I promise I will not give it back in ruin. It will not be ripped or shredded. I know there have been times that you have been disappointed with the result of your efforts, but I want you to know how proud I am of you.

You do not have to wrestle with LIFE. You just have to receive it. My heart is full and it is bursting with love for you. Be still and know that I am God.

Stand underneath me while I wash over you like a waterfall. See, I love you and there is nothing I want more than for you to get rid of every entanglement. I want to see you rise up and stand firm. Call on my name, for I am your strong tower. Run to me and find the strength you need.

No soldier in active service gets entangled in the [ordinary business] affairs of civilian life; [he avoids them] so that he may please the one who enlisted him to serve.
– 2 TIMOTHY 2:4

September 30

BE CONFIDENT IN ME AND IN WHAT I CAN DO. I am working the ground beneath your feet. Do not despise the pace I have you on. The world's wisdom is not my wisdom. For the world knows self-ambition and will do whatever it can do to achieve its own end. Do not crave riches. Instead crave abundant LIFE, for my kingdom is set up to deliver everything your heart cries for.

I will set before you the desires of your heart. I have not forgotten about the things I have promised you. I have many things for you that I am working out even right now. Be confident in who you are, who I am in you, and the gifts I have given you. Be glad today; make a joyful noise and give me a shout.

For with God nothing [is or ever] shall be impossible.

– LUKE 1:37

This page intentionally left blank

October

Also it is not good for a person to be without knowledge, and he who hurries with his feet [acting impulsively and proceeding without caution or analyzing the consequences] sins (misses the mark).

– PROVERBS 19:2

October 1

I AM INFUSING LIFE INTO EVERYTHING around you. Everything you are involved in will bring forth LIFE. Just be patient and let me work for you. Be sensitive to my spirit and do not let your excitement drown out my voice. Do not run ahead with every new wave of thinking or ideas. Stay grounded with me.

Exalt my love and lift up my heart. That is so important; I am so happy you seek to do that. My love in you becomes real for others when they listen to you and watch what you do. My love is the message and song of your heart.

I am the source of LIFE and am actively pursuing you. I will not relent in my passionate pursuit of you.

Also it is not good for a person to be without knowledge, and he who hurries with his feet [acting impulsively and proceeding without caution or analyzing the consequences] sins (misses the mark).

– PROVERBS 19:2

October 2

I WILL QUENCH YOUR THIRST. I am the only one who can. I am sharing my heart with you. Listen. It is a beautiful melody. Do you hear it?

You have a home – a place to rest. It is in my heart. I love you so much; my heart is bursting for you. Your passions are my passions.

I have marked out this day for you. Stay by my side and we will walk together today and every day. Like toothpicks scattered across the ground, so are the opportunities that are coming your way. I will organize and keep them together. Do not be overwhelmed. I am with you and my strength is for you. I am the well of LIFE that will never dry up.

From the end of the earth I call to You, when my heart is overwhelmed and weak; lead me to the rock that is higher than I [a rock that is too high to reach without Your help]. For You have been a shelter and a refuge for me, a strong tower against the enemy. Let me dwell in Your tent forever; let me take refuge in the shelter of Your wings. Selah.

– PSALM 61:2-4

October 3

I LOVE YOU. I have so many things for you to be excited about. Let me color your eyes and spark LIFE into your heart. The clouds will clear away and sunlight is going to break through. You are my mighty child. I am with you.

I love you. Mountains move when you speak my words. Strongholds of the enemy shutter and fail because of my words that flow from your mouth. Those on the receiving end are deeply impacted – physically, spiritually, and emotionally.

Do not fold to the pressure to do more than you are comfortable with. Listen to me; I will help you decide if you have the ability to add more to your schedule.

So the people shouted [the battle cry], and the priests blew the trumpets. When the people heard the sound of the trumpet, they raised a great shout and the wall [of Jericho] fell down, so that the sons of Israel went up into the city, every man straight ahead [climbing over the rubble], and they overthrew the city.
– JOSHUA 6:20

October 4

BEHOLD, I AM DOING A NEW THING in your life. Do not ever get tired of hearing that. Every day is a new adventure for us to walk in together. I am always leading you into promotion and elevation.

Do not assume you know what I am going to say before I say it. Do not confine me to that box. The truth is that you need to be reminded of the words I have spoken to you in the past, and of their meaning.

I am the light that switches on in your heart. I illuminate everything, and then release my words into the space. My words will never return void; they will never leave things unchanged. They will accomplish what I have intended for them to do.

Therefore humble yourselves under the mighty hand of God [set aside self-righteous pride], so that He may exalt you [to a place of honor in His service] at the appropriate time.

– 1 PETER 5:6

So will My word be which goes out of My mouth; it will not return to Me void (useless, without result), without accomplishing what I desire, and without succeeding in the matter for which I sent it.

– ISIAH 55:11

October 5

LET MY PURITY WASH OVER YOU and cleanse your mind. I am bright and holy. Fashion yourself after me – be holy as I am holy. Desire what is good and flee from what is evil. I have prepared a place for you. It is here with me; recline with me; you are never alone; loneliness is a lie.

My light produces LIFE. You were created to be alive in me. I am hope and I am peace. I am the door at the end of a dark tunnel. See the light creeping in around the frame? Throw it open, step into my presence, and be lifted high in my arms.

You are my delight. I have a song I made just for you. It is always on my lips. Keep your heart soft. Do not let it harden based on who you happen to be around. Continue to open your heart to those around you, for my love pours out from yours.

But like the Holy One who called you, be holy yourselves in all your conduct [be set apart from the world by your godly character and moral courage]; because it is written, "You shall be holy (set apart), for I am holy."

– 1 PETER 1:15-16

October 6

LAY YOUR HEAD ON MY SHOULDER. It is okay; everything is going to be fine. Just keep moving with me. Power and authority flows from my heart to yours, from my presence to yours. Use it. Know who you are and who I am in you. The storms of the world swirl overhead, but I am peace. The clouds will part to reveal a new day. Have fun in it.

Your head will always have a place on my chest. Feel my breath on your neck and listen to the beat of my heart. It is steady; it never fails. I am unfolding the plans that I have for you and for the dreams you have held in your heart. I told you that I would give you the desires of your heart. I am not one that should lie. I will do all that I say I will do. Have faith and confidence in me. I care deeply about the things you want and desire. I will provide the things that you need. The path is marked out for you. Follow it.

For His anger is but for a moment, His favor is for a lifetime. Weeping may endure for a night, but a shout of joy comes in the morning.

– PSALM 30:5

October 7

THERE ARE THINGS COMING that will seem to shake the ground you are standing on. Do not be afraid. It is the nature of progress. There is no moving forward without a little bit of shaking. But it is not negative or destructive if I am the one moving you forward.

Anxiety and fear are what the shaking is. But you do not have to be afraid; even in the discomfort, I am God. I am your redeemer and deliverer. I am your healer and provider. Be patient and wait for me. Move with confidence through the doors I open. Do not try to pick the lock of the doors that are shut. There are some that are shut now that will open later.

I am still teaching you. Do not despise my correction. Stay open to my voice of instruction as I lead you into areas you are not familiar with. Do not shut out counsel.

We are pressured in every way [hedged in], but not crushed; perplexed [unsure of finding a way out], but not driven to despair; hunted down and persecuted, but not deserted [to stand alone]; struck down, but never destroyed; always carrying around in the body the dying of Jesus, so that the [resurrection] life of Jesus also may be shown in our body.
– 2 CORINTHIANS 4:8-10

October 8

IN THE MIDST OF WAVES ROARING and crashing all around you, I am the gentle breeze that reminds you peace can exist in any circumstance. You just have to look for it.

Command the storms around you to be still. Everything may not suddenly align perfectly, but you will enter into rest. "*Peace be still*" is more about you than it is about the external circumstances. It is about your ability to remain in peace despite the storms that come. It is about your ability to be still and know that I am God and that I am working for you.

Remember, if I am for you, who or what can stand against you? Only those things that you believe are more powerful will have the ability to stand in your way.

Even though I walk through the [sunless] valley of the shadow of death, I fear no evil, for You are with me; Your rod [to protect] and Your staff [to guide], they comfort and console me. You prepare a table before me in the presence of my enemies. You have anointed and refreshed my head with oil; my cup overflows.

– PSALM 23:4-5

October 9

WHAT DO YOU THINK IS *DOING* ENOUGH? Do a little extra and the voice of the enemy will only tell you that you should be doing more. If you are going to do more, it cannot be an attempt to silence the voice of accusation, because that will never work. The imaginary bar will only be lifted higher.

Consider a cabinet full of spices. I am full of all sorts of flavors. When your foundation is LIFE, the things you enjoy enhance that LIFE. But if your foundation is death, the spices I carry can only mask the stench.

Let my love for you be your foundation. If you do, the joys that come will be enhancers instead of temporary distractions.

Let us therefore make every effort to enter that rest [of God, to know and experience it for ourselves], so that no one will fall by following the same example of disobedience [as those who died in the wilderness].

– HEBREWS 4:11

❡ *October 10* ❦

YOU ARE A LABOR OF MY LOVE. It gives me joy to work with you, and in you, to bring forth everything I planted from the first days you were formed. It is my breath that gives LIFE to the things lying dormant inside of my kids. My words are water. My body is the shade to keep it from being scorched.

I love you so much. Look at me and understand who I am. Do not look to your own understanding, but let me change and transform your thinking into my own thoughts and processes.

For we are God's fellow workers [His servants working together]; you are God's cultivated field [His garden, His vineyard], God's building.

– 1 CORINTHIANS 3:9

"Before I formed you in the womb I knew you [and approved of you as My chosen instrument], and before you were born I consecrated you [to Myself as My own]; I have appointed you as a prophet to the nations."

– JEREMIAH 1:5

October 11

INACTIVITY IS A WEAPON OF YOUR ADVERSARY.

There is a difference between rest, and stopping completely. Rest can happen no matter what is going on around you – no matter what you happen to be doing. It is a place of peace inside of my heart that transcends all other activities.

You are a transformer. When you are in step with me, everything you do changes the world in way that brings LIFE. We are doing it together. You are a transformer because I have transformed you.

My light shines brightest when you are standing in the dark. That is why your adversary tries to fill you with false light and wash mine out. If people do not know that they are in darkness, they will never notice my light. Make sure that they notice by being a reflection of my heart. I am holding you closely. Do not become weary of doing good.

Do this, knowing that this is a critical time. It is already the hour for you to awaken from your sleep [of spiritual complacency]; for our salvation is nearer to us now than when we first believed [in Christ]. The night [this present evil age] is almost gone and the day [of Christ's return] is almost here. So let us fling away the works of darkness and put on the [full] armor of light.

– ROMANS 13:11-12

October 12

I HAVE CALLED YOU TO HELP PEOPLE SEE and understand me. Your very presence helps open the eyes of those standing in darkness. Lead them to me and I will lead them to the cross.

I love you so much. You can be so consumed by my love and peace that it feels like you are gliding, even as butterflies float through the air. When you rely on me, there is nothing that can cause anxiety or worry. In me is the absence of fear.

Your day is in my hands. Trust me with it. Take my hand and I will lead you step by step. Do not let your to-do list control you. Do not let it drive and consume you. Will you let me help?

Incline Your ear to me, deliver me quickly; be my rock of refuge, and a strong fortress to save me. Yes, You are my rock and my fortress; for Your name's sake You will lead me and guide me.

– PSALM 31:2-3

October 13

THE MORE YOU RUN INTO MY ARMS, the more you will detest sin. You will find LIFE in one and death in the other. Sin will lose whatever attraction it once held.

When the hope of LIFE is drained, the attraction is gone. The only things sin can provide are the temporary distractions you sometimes want. But the consequences of those temporary distractions can be long lasting, and sometimes permanent.

But I have overcome. I restore and I redeem. There is nothing that has been stolen from you that would be impossible for me to return. My heart is shining bright for you like a lamppost or a lantern. It not only draws you to me, but then it also shows you the way in which you should walk. Step into the river of my LIFE and you will be consumed.

Who is the one who is victorious and overcomes the world? It is the one who believes and recognizes the fact that Jesus is the Son of God.

– 1 JOHN 5:5

October 14

I AM MOVING IN YOUR LIFE like a street sweeper. I am even lifting off the manhole covers and inspecting the sewers. It does not matter what is running through them because I will clean everything up.

Nothing can be hidden down there anyway. There have been times that you have tried, but each time the stench wandered up and out into the street. The things that stain hearts cannot be pushed down and forgotten. Eventually they will affect everything you say and do.

But there is no stain that can stand against the cleansing power of my perfect love. I have an ocean of grace and mercy waiting to saturate your heart and let you know that it is going to be okay. You can forgive yourself because I have already forgiven you. Do not listen to the lies of shame, guilt, and condemnation. You are free, and it is time for you to accept that I really am that good, and that I really do love you that much.

"Come now, and let us reason together," says the Lord. "Though your sins are like scarlet, they shall be as white as snow; though they are red like crimson, they shall be like wool.

– ISAIAH 1:18

October 15

MANAGE MY WORDS WITH LOVE. I will love others through the way you interact and speak with them. It is important to me that they be treated right. There are times that it is more difficult to treat people with love and honor, but those are the times in which you have the opportunity to grow. That is promotion; that is maturing and advancing. Pay attention to the opportunities to be my reflection to the world. You are already doing that in so many ways. I am pleased with you.

I am tending you, pruning you like a precious flower in my garden. I am the gardener. I am so attentive to the needs of every plant established here. My goal is that they all produce fruit.

There is an extra element in my garden – the element of free will. All conditions can be perfect, and yet little to no growth happens. In my garden, the plants have a choice to grow.

But I say to you, love [unselfishly seek the best or higher good for] your enemies and pray for those who persecute you, so that you may [show yourselves to] be the children of your Father who is in heaven.

– MATTHEW 5:44-45

October 16

I WANT YOU TO ALWAYS PRAY and contend for me to release my words into your life.

I am doing a new thing in you. Let me move you forward into it. Take my hand and watch your footsteps create LIFE wherever they fall. You are breeching the walls that have previously held you back. Stay with me as you enter into the new things I have prepared for you. It is not time to run; it is time to match my pace.

I cannot wait to reveal the things I have for you. I am like a child on Christmas morning who is unable to contain their excitement. My intention is to always bring incredibly good things into your life. It is my heart for you, so I work to that aim. Do not allow the shining lights that the world has to offer pull you away from me.

For the Lord God is a sun and shield; the Lord bestows grace and favor and honor; no good thing will He withhold from those who walk uprightly.

– PSALM 84:11

October 17

I WANT YOU TO ALWAYS BE FREE to hope and dream, but do not let those hopes and dreams rule you. Let *me* reign in you.

My beloved child, I am turning the wheel and gears. They are the innards of a clock and the clock is displaying the timing I have for you. The timing is deliberate and full of purpose. Do not try to speed it up; rather, wait until the appointed hour.

Rest in me; let me swallow you up in my goodness. Surely goodness and righteousness are forever attached to me. And I am in you, so they are attached to you as well. All you have to do is rest and receive. My peace is the best kind of sedative – all of the peace without the drugs.

Let the peace of Christ [the inner calm of one who walks daily with Him] be the controlling factor in your hearts [deciding and settling questions that arise]. To this peace indeed you were called as members in one body [of believers]. And be thankful [to God always].

– COLOSSIANS 3:15

October 18

I HAVE A SCRAPBOOK RESERVED for the days ahead. I plan to fill it with all of our moments of joy, laughter, and delight. It will be a very thick book. There are many of these moments ahead.

The work that you are doing is bringing LIFE. Do not focus only on what you can see, but consider the work being done that is unseen. Like workers who strike oil, so are you striking LIFE and uncovering it for those who are desperate for me. They are coming alive. Keep moving forward in what I have called you to do. You are qualified; you are making a difference; you are a positive impact.

Listen to my voice instead of the one shouting discouragement.

For the kingdom of God is not based on talk but on power

– CORINTHIANS 4:20

October 19

I LOVE YOU SO MUCH. I never look at you with disgust in my eyes. You will only find love there. You are not alone; I am right here. I have not run away in frustration. My heart, patience, and longsuffering is greater, and more intense, than you can imagine.

I am here because I love and adore you, even when you get muddy and covered with much of the world. I will pick you up, clean your wounds, and get you ready to face the new day.

Now, let's move forward into all that I have for you. Step out of shame, guilt and condemnation into my love, into my light. Abundant LIFE is not something that expires because of what you do or do not do. It will always be available to you.

But You, O Lord, are a God [who protects and is] merciful and gracious, slow to anger and abounding in lovingkindness and truth.

– PSALM 86:15

October 20

I AM THE HEALER OF YOUR BODY, soul, and spirit. I have come to remove the cloak of heaviness. I have already prepared for you a beautiful garment of praise. Will you hand me the cloak of heaviness and let me replace it? It is my desire to see you healed and free. Walk with me and you will see a deeper healing and freedom than you ever thought was possible.

We can walk straight through the battlefield when you stay by my side. There is no need to hide in the trenches. Freedom is walking into the onslaught with confidence of your safety. That freedom comes from being in my presence.

'For I will restore health to you and I will heal your wounds,' says the Lord, 'Because they have called you an outcast, saying: "This is Zion; no one seeks her and no one cares for her." '

– JEREMIAH 30:17

October 21

ONE OF THE HARDEST THINGS for my kids to do is look at me through clear eyes when they have fallen. How quickly they can revert back to what they have known their whole lives. Some of the greatest testimonies of transformation come when you realize who I am in the midst of your failures.

I am the light in your eyes. You cannot get rid of me. Shake off the dirt, take a shower, and join me in the fullness I have to offer. Did you know that no matter how much a person is walking in darkness, I can see things in them that make me smile? If I can bring those things out, the darkness will fade. Keep running into my love.

If we [freely] admit that we have sinned and confess our sins, He is faithful and just [true to His own nature and promises], and will forgive our sins and cleanse us continually from all unrighteousness [our wrongdoing, everything not in conformity with His will and purpose].

– 1 JOHN 1:9

October 22

LEAVE THE OLD BEHIND and press on to the new. I am preparing, and have prepared, many things for you. They lie ahead; I do not work in the past. I work in the present and prepare for the future.

Those who run to me will be saved. I am a fortress, a strong tower. I have come that you may have victory over the things holding you back. I have placed the tools of freedom in your hands. Move forward and I will destroy the chains that hold you. I am pouring my abundant LIFE into a cup just for you. Drink it all and you will be filled to overflowing.

'The latter glory of this house will be greater than the former,' says the Lord of hosts, 'and in this place I shall give [the ultimate] peace and prosperity,' declares the Lord of hosts."

– HAGGAI 2:9

October 23

I LOVE YOU. You are like the ripest apple hanging on the branch. My eyes caught you from afar and I have been captivated ever since. The inner workings of your heart are entwined with my fingers. You have allowed me into who you are, and so my heart is mixed with yours. There is so much LIFE in you because I am in you. And I will be in you in increasing degrees.

I know you have felt that the work of your hands is not producing the fruit you want it to. Do not let what you can see become your only reality. I do not measure impact by numbers. Seek first the advancement of my kingdom and everything else will be added to you.

For thus says the Lord of hosts, "After glory He has sent Me against the nations which plunder you—for he who touches you, touches the apple of His eye."

– ZECHARIAH 2:8

October 24

YOU ARE AWESOME; YOU MAKE ME GIGGLE. Let my wisdom light your way. The spirit of wisdom and revelation is a gift from me. When you allow it into your heart, you can see clearly.

I love you and am making a way for you. Trust what I am doing in your life. Sometimes my kids ask me for wonderful things, and I want to give those things to them, but they lack the foresight to know how it could negatively affect them.

I am protecting you. You would be shocked to discover how many times the enemy has used opportunities that seem great to break down even the strongest people. Listen to my voice of direction. I will lead you where you want to go. I can say that because I know you want the things of my heart. Be confident in my love for you.

Consider and answer me, O Lord my God; give light (life) to my eyes, or I will sleep the sleep of death, and my enemy will say, "I have overcome him," and my adversaries will rejoice when I am shaken. But I have trusted and relied on and been confident in Your lovingkindness and faithfulness; my heart shall rejoice and delight in Your salvation.

– PSALM 13:3-5

October 25

STRIVING TO ENTER MY REST looks like letting go. Striving typically means holding on even tighter. However, entering my rest means letting go. Release all of your worries and just fall into my arms. The more you let go, the more you enter my rest. It can feel like work at times because the natural inclination is to control – to do things your self. It takes an active choice to let me have your cares and concerns.

There is no condemnation for you unless you let condemnation gain access to your heart. Be diligent against the voice of accusation against you. Bring your questions to me. I have positioned wise counsel around you that you can ask if you are having trouble hearing from me. That is why community is so important. Let the people around you speak LIFE into your heart.

Therefore there is now no condemnation [no guilty verdict, no punishment] for those who are in Christ Jesus [who believe in Him as personal Lord and Savior].

– ROMANS 8:1

❧ *October 26* ❧

I AM A RIVER OF LIFE IN YOU. I am a fountain of blessing. Release that water to the world around you. I am alive and active right now beside you. There are things happening all around that you cannot see. That is why you must trust in me. Do not forget the things I have told you. Do not lose confidence in my promises. If you remain steadfast, the choices you make will lead you to the Promised Land.

When you lose confidence in me, you start trying to bring about the results on your own. That is when my plans get messed up. If you trust in me, there is no need to try to make things happen on your own.

Trust that the ripples of what you are doing are going out and accomplishing great things. Let me manage the big splashes. I know what needs to be done and I am doing it.

But Jesus answered them, "My Father has been working until now [He has never ceased working], and I too am working."
– JOHN 5:17

October 27

I LOVE IT WHEN WE SPEND TIME TOGETHER. It does not have to be for any specific length of time. Even the short times we spend together are important to me.

I hold you with an open hand to let you make the decisions and choices you want, but with a closed hand when it comes to my love. I will never let you go.

I am a refreshing waterfall on your ragged, weary body. Those in the desert cry out and are saved by the flood of LIFE I bring. Those lost in the desert are who I came for. I came to draw them to my side.

But the news about Him was spreading farther, and large crowds kept gathering to hear Him and to be healed of their illnesses. But Jesus Himself would often slip away to the wilderness and pray [in seclusion].

– LUKE 5:15-16

October 28

YOU, THOUGH ONCE LOST IN THE DESERT, are now walking by my side through the Promised Land. It does not mean you do not experience trials, but it means that you have understood your access to my LIFE. I am the Promised Land. I am milk and honey. I am where all promises are fulfilled. The Promised Land goes with you wherever you go.

Travel deeper into me. My well stretches farther than you know; dig until you strike oil. I have placed my words in your mouth; they are richer than oil to the thirsty soul. They make the recipient richer than the greatest treasure the world has to offer. In the world, one can be rich and poor at the same time, but with me, one can only be rich.

For as many as are the promises of God, in Christ they are [all answered] "Yes." So through Him we say our "Amen" to the glory of God.

– 2 CORINTHIANS 1:20

October 29

I AM THE LIFE, THE TRUTH, AND THE WAY. I light up the darkness. There is no need to remain in the shadows. Step out of the darkness and into my presence. I have come to eliminate the shadows and to help my children realize that they are of the light. Freedom comes when you realize that you do not need to hide your face.

There is nothing you could experience that I have not already experienced. I know what pain is. I know what it is to suffer. I have been through it and I can help you manage any situation you find yourself in. You are not alone!

For we do not have a High Priest who is unable to sympathize and understand our weaknesses and temptations, but One who has been tempted [knowing exactly how it feels to be human] in every respect as we are, yet without [committing any] sin.

– HEBREWS 4:15

October 30

KEEP YOUR EYES ON WHAT IS AHEAD. You cannot live while striving to return to the past. Live for *this* moment, and then the next. I cannot establish you in the past, but I can set your feet in the present. Our journey forward is a new one. The old is old; let it go. What I am doing in you now will be greater than anything in the past. I will take care of you. You do not need to be afraid. I am with you.

Be content with where I have you right now. Rest in it. Protect the joy that is trying to burst forth. Guard and protect it against the schemes of the enemy. Live in me and live in peace.

"Do not remember the former things, or ponder the things of the past. "Listen carefully, I am about to do a new thing, now it will spring forth; will you not be aware of it? I will even put a road in the wilderness, rivers in the desert."

– ISAIAH 43:18-19

October 31

IT IS AN AMAZING THING when my kids lift their eyes to me. There are so many different things vying for your attention, so when you draw your eyes to me I feel like there are a million fireworks exploding in the air. Keep your eyes on me. Do not be drawn away by the distractions of the world. They will try to pull you away. It is not easy to stand firm. It will take courage and strength to accomplish this.

I am right here with you. Do not be anxious about anything but in all things present your needs before me. Do not go into *autopilot* when I quote scripture to you. If you present your needs to me, you will be able to release them. But you have to trust in my love before you can release your worries. Will you trust that I love you enough to take care of you?

Unto you I lift up my eyes, O You who are enthroned in the heavens! Behold, as the eyes of servants look to the hand of their master, and as the eyes of a maid to the hand of her mistress, so our eyes look to the Lord our God, until He is gracious and favorable toward us.

– PSALM 123:1-2

November

May our God come and not keep silent;
fire devours before Him, and around
Him a mighty tempest rages.

– PSALM 50:3

November 1

SOMETIMES THE THOUGHTS in your head tie everything up in knots. Relax! Let go of it all and let me take it. I will unravel the things that have become twisted for you.

Splash down into my waters. Feel how light you are; float without any burdens. Let my peace fill you now. Let it overwhelm and overtake you. There is nothing you need to worry about; I have it all in my mind. Listen to me; inquire of me. I will not be silent. I will not stand idly by and observe from the sidelines. I am an active participant. I am on your team. Let me help you.

May our God come and not keep silent; fire devours before Him, and around Him a mighty tempest rages.

– PSALM 50:3

Therefore My people shall know My Name and what it means. Therefore in that day I am the One who is speaking, 'Here I am.'

– ISAIAH 53:6

❧ November 2 ❧

THERE IS NO NEED TO ACHIEVE IN MY PRESENCE.

In my presence, you are everything I want you to be. You are the fullest you could ever be when you are in my presence.

Do not ever lose hope. As long as there is hope, there is a spark, no matter how difficult things might be. That spark is all I need to work with. I am the one who attends to the fire and stokes it as needed.

Enjoy me. I really enjoy you. I love your smile and your tender heart. We have traveled a long way and the journey is not over. I have formed you into my image. The doors are before you and are just now beginning to open in a new way. The stage is set. Do not be afraid. I am on the stage with you.

[You are the One] who covers Yourself with light as with a garment, who stretches out the heavens like a tent curtain, who lays the beams of His upper chambers in the waters [above the firmament], who makes the clouds His chariot, who walks on the wings of the wind, who makes winds His messengers, flames of fire His ministers.

– PSALM 104:2-4

❧ *November 3* ❧

COME AND LOOK WITH ME. Consider a beautiful little pond full of lily pads and surrounded by lush, green foliage. Watch how the tadpoles gather at the surface when I reach my hand over the water. My creation brings me so much joy. It is my desire that you would experience joy in the little things as well. Freedom in me increases your ability to do this. Shrug off the cloak of oppression and run through the fields with abandon.

I will show you things that will make your eyes grow wide with wonder. My kingdom is a paradise beyond your wildest dreams or expectations. Nothing compares to its beauty.

God saw everything that He had made, and behold, it was very good and He validated it completely.

– GENESIS 1:31

Call to Me and I will answer you, and tell you [and even show you] great and mighty things, [things which have been confined and hidden], which you do not know and understand and cannot distinguish.

– JEREMIAH 33:3

November 4

MY WORDS ARE HONEY ON YOUR LIPS. Let them be a sweet taste in your mouth. Do not let my words become bitter to you. Do not scrunch up your nose at the revelation I bring. I have come to set you free and you will be free in even greater ways than you are now.

I love you so much. You are more precious than the largest diamond. Let your eyes see what I am showing you. I am your leader, your redeemer, and your bridegroom. I love you and am continually filling you with my joy and presence. Open yourself up to me. Take off the lid of your heart and let me pour my presence into it.

The precepts of the Lord are right, bringing joy to the heart; the commandment of the Lord is pure, enlightening the eyes. The fear of the Lord is clean, enduring forever; The judgments of the Lord are true, they are righteous altogether. They are more desirable than gold, yes, than much fine gold; sweeter also than honey and the drippings of the honeycomb.

– PSALM 19:8-10

November 5

LIE DOWN IN MY COOL WATERS and I will flow over you. Let my heart be the place where you settle. I will meet you there. I will feed you and instruct you in the ways of my kingdom.

Wake up! The parts of you that are slumbering need to wake up to my voice. Let every cell be inspired. Let every cell awaken right now to the sound of my voice. I have come to bring LIFE to every part of your being.

Do not give in to discouragement. Stand strong against it. I will give you the energy and strength you need to overcome. But you must continue to stand.

The Lord is my Shepherd [to feed, to guide and to shield me], I shall not want. He lets me lie down in green pastures; He leads me beside the still and quiet waters. He refreshes and restores my soul (life); He leads me in the paths of righteousness for His name's sake.

– PSALM 23:1-3

❧ *November 6* ❧

MY SPIRIT OF WISDOM IS ALWAYS AVAILABLE for those who will seek it. There are two seemingly identical mountains – the world and my kingdom. Though at times they look similar, their purposes are drastically different. Trust me for direction. I will lead and guide you, keeping you safe from the counterfeit mountain. False mountain top experiences are deceiving my people. They are being drawn by the promise of instant fulfillment but discover the emptiness of that pursuit.

The world can only offer temporary fulfillment. It only leads to craving more. It is a never ending circular pursuit filled with starvation. My kingdom can offer constant contentment and peace in every moment. Seek my wisdom and enjoy the climb with me.

If any of you lacks wisdom [to guide him through a decision or circumstance], he is to ask of [our benevolent] God, who gives to everyone generously and without rebuke or blame, and it will be given to him.

– JAMES 1:5

November 7

THERE IS NO CONDEMNATION for you as you are in me. I am not holding guilt over your head, so do not let the enemy hang it there. You are full of love. You are not perfect, but I smile because perfection was never something I demanded. What did I ask? Be just, love kindness, and walk humbly with me. "Be perfect," is not included. You are not perfect, but you are perfectly accepted, adored, and loved.

He has told you, O man, what is good; and what does the Lord require of you except to be just, and to love [and to diligently practice] kindness (compassion), and to walk humbly with your God [setting aside any overblown sense of importance or self-righteousness]?

– MICAH 6:8

November 8

I HEAR EVERY CRY FROM THE SAVED and unsaved alike. Every voice reaches my ears. How I long to bring relief to every kind of suffering. All day long I hold out my hand; those who reach back are helped while those who do not sink deeper into despair.

Sometimes my hand means instant healing or deliverance; at other times it is something to hold onto as we walk the path that needs to be walked. It varies because circumstances vary. But one thing remains true in any situation – I will lead you to redemption; I will lead you to freedom. But you must take the steps I ask you to take. Not because I am a vindictive, controlling master, but because I know the path that will take you to freedom and healing. Follow me because I know the way.

You have taken account of my wanderings; put my tears in Your bottle. Are they not recorded in Your book? Then my enemies will turn back in the day when I call; this I know, that God is for me. In God, whose word I praise, in the Lord, whose word I praise, in God have I put my trust and confident reliance; I will not be afraid. What can man do to me?

– PSALM 56:8-11

November 9

I SIT ON THE THRONE OF POWER AND MIGHT; my love extends and touches everything. I am both the lion and the lamb. My lion qualities express my passionate and intense love. My lamb traits represent my humility and servant's heart. I am not a harsh ruler; in fact, I invite questions and wonderings. I will explain and I will teach, for I am the good shepherd. I am the good teacher.

Come and share your heart with me. Do not be afraid of coming to me with your doubts. Let me help you come to the conclusion. I am a patient father and will work diligently with you. I love to see you learn and grow. I long to give you new revelation and truth, but I will never force you beyond what you are ready to handle.

In the year that King Uzziah died, I saw [in a vision] the Lord sitting on a throne, high and exalted, with the train of His royal robe filling the [most holy part of the] temple.

– ISAIAH 6:1

November 10

KEEP PURSUING MY HEART. If our relationship has grown stale, it is not because of me. It is because you have stopped pressing into me. You will never reach the bottom of who I am; there is always more to find. The things I have for you are exciting, and I want you to discover them.

Get your hardhat and pickaxe and start digging into the greater riches of my heart. You will meet resistance; not from me, but from your adversary. He will try to drain your energy and courage. He will try to discourage you. Press in and listen only to my voice. You are royalty; I have established you.

Light is sown [like seed] for the righteous and illuminates their path, and [irrepressible] joy [is spread] for the upright in heart [who delight in His favor and protection].

– PSALM 97:11

❧ *November 11* ❧

YES, I AM HERE WITH YOU. My presence is electric. Let my river of peace flow through you as you fall into my arms. Let me take you and consume you. Everything is going to be okay because I am with you and I am for you.

You might be staring at a closed door, but I can see the other side. Be content with where you are. Take a look at all of the blessings around you. Get excited about what you have right now. You have me, and will always have me. This awareness will bring light into the darkest day. Discouragement cannot stand against this revelation.

Just rest in my arms and stop living in the future. Do not live in tomorrow. Live in this moment with me. Remember what joy is; remember that you are the sparkle in my eye. I will never forsake my bride.

So do not worry about tomorrow; for tomorrow will worry about itself. Each day has enough trouble of its own.

– MATTHEW 6:34

November 12

I AM HERE. Seek me and you will find my kingdom. Let the pursuit of my kingdom be your highest aim. I love you and would move heaven and earth for you. Receive that, for I speak truth. Deceit is not in me and has no part of me. I *am* truth; I do not lead anyone astray.

The truth of who I am is LOVE. My love is the glue that holds all things together. Everything would crumble without it. Meditate on this, for this truth will bring you LIFE.

We have come to know [by personal observation and experience], and have believed [with deep, consistent faith] the love which God has for us. God is love, and the one who abides in love abides in God, and God abides continually in him.

– 1 JOHN 4:16

November 13

IT IS GOING TO BE OKAY. I am with you. Feel my arms around you. Be real about what you are feeling, but do not give fear a foothold. Do not be afraid to express concern or emotion. Remember that I have overcome. Plant my LIFE within you and watch it grow.

Revelation is like the best steak you have ever eaten. It is meat for those who are hungry and will fill you until you are ready for more. It needs to be processed and digested before understanding can come. Wait for the understanding before you begin to share it with others.

I am lighting the way for you. The impact of where I am taking you will be beyond what you can imagine, but I do not want you focusing on that. I just want you to follow me. I will help you to be prepared, but do not live in the future. Exist with me in the present.

But Mary treasured all these things, giving careful thought to them and pondering them in her heart.

– LUKE 2:19

Do not give that which is holy to dogs, and do not throw your pearls before pigs, for they will trample them under their feet, and turn and tear you to pieces.

– MATTHEW 7:6

November 14

I LOVE YOU AND WILL LEAD YOU. Do not worry, because it is going to be ok. I am your security, wisdom, and revelation. I will make a way for you even in desert land. Wait on me; be patient. Be still and know that I am God and that I care about what you care about.

Lead others into LIFE. Do not become an offense to the people around you. Let my purity wash over you and cleanse everything you are. I am bright and holy. Let me fashion you into my image. Desire what is good and flee from what is evil.

Do not offend Jews or Greeks or even the church of God [but live to honor Him]; just as I please everyone in all things [as much as possible adapting myself to the interests of others], not seeking my own benefit but that of the many, so that they [will be open to the message of salvation and] may be saved.

– 1 CORINTHIANS 10:32-33

November 15

I HAVE OVERCOME THE WORLD. I have won. Rejoice in what I have already done. Satan has lost. Together we have victory – victory over anything and everything that seeks to kill and destroy. Yes, even over death. I have given you the power to overcome.

I see my children labeled as overcomers, as victors. Take the spoils of that victory. You are not a victim. Satan is a cowering dog lying in the shadows truly scared of those who have overcome through me. He knows he holds no power over them and stands to lose even more as they go forth into the harvest. His kingdom is decreasing. Mine is ever increasing!

When He had disarmed the rulers and authorities [those supernatural forces of evil operating against us], He made a public example of them [exhibiting them as captives in His triumphal procession], having triumphed over them through the cross.

– COLOSSIANS 2:15

November 16

I LOVE YOU SO MUCH. You are so precious to me. My heart beats for you. I am the one who can lift you out of the mud of your transgressions and purify you with my love and righteousness. You are clean and pure, and I find no fault in you. You are my spotless bride. Walk in that knowledge; rest in it.

It is not that you are perfect, but rather that I love you perfectly. There is no shadow of changing in me. I am constant, a constant ray of love and light. Though you may walk at times through the valleys, I will light your way and help you find rest. Trust in me.

There shall be no end to the increase of His government and of peace, [He shall rule] on the throne of David and over his kingdom, to establish it and to uphold it with justice and righteousness from that time forward and forevermore. The zeal of the Lord of hosts will accomplish this.

– ISAIAH 9:7

November 17

YOU DO NOT FULLY UNDERSTAND my ability and desire to give you the things you need and even want. But that is okay. If you are willing to step out with me, you will learn. I know the desires of your heart and I want to provide them for you.

Do not mistake one way for the only way. I see many different ways that you do not. Trust in what I can do. Be confident in me. Remember the times I have provided for you in the past. Do not let what you cannot see tell you that what you want or need is impossible. With me all things are possible.

I love you so much and have so much planned for you. Keep walking with me and follow my footsteps. I am not hiding the way from you. I want you to be happy.

I know that there is nothing better for them than to rejoice and to do good as long as they live; and also that every man should eat and drink and see and enjoy the good of all his labor—it is the gift of God.

– ECCLESIASTES 3:12-13

November 18

BE A WORSHIPER. Live in such a way that your very presence ushers in my love. You do this so often, and when you do, people take notice. You stand out amidst the darkness and shine so brightly. The more you are in, and aware of, my presence, the more your heart will look like mine.

Pursue my heart and you shall live under the shadow of my wings forever. I will gather you under me like a hen gathers her chicks. You will always have a place to rest your head, for I have you in the center of my hand. My gaze is ever on you.

O come, let us worship and bow down, let us kneel before the Lord our Maker [in reverent praise and prayer].

– PSALM 95:6

November 19

MY FINGERPRINTS ARE ON YOU. I love you; my love covers every part of you. I will pour through your home like rushing water. I will flood the air with my presence and come down in a cloud. My heavenly host has surrounded you. You have made a dwelling place for me in your heart.

I love you and am with you. Seek me and you will always find me. Pursue my heart and it will open up to you. I will never turn you away. You are my beloved child and I am your big daddy. Cast your cares on me, for I care for you. I will provide all of your needs.

Oh, that You would tear open the heavens and come down, that the mountains might quake at Your presence—

– ISAIAH 64:1

November 20

I HAVE PREPARED A PLACE FOR YOU here in my presence. Come and recline with me. Listen to, and feel, my heart beat for you. I am always here. You are never alone. Choose to walk in my light because my light produces LIFE.

I am the pleasing fragrance in your nostrils. I am what makes your heart whole. You were created to be alive in me. I am hope and I am peace. I am the deliverer of those who are in bonds. I am the door at the end of a dark tunnel. See the light creeping in around the frame. Throw it open, step into my presence, and be lifted high in my arms.

You are my delight. I have a song I created just for you. It is always on my lips.

But if we [really] walk in the Light [that is, live each and every day in conformity with the precepts of God], as He Himself is in the Light, we have [true, unbroken] fellowship with one another [He with us, and we with Him], and the blood of Jesus His Son cleanses us from all sin [by erasing the stain of sin, keeping us cleansed from sin in all its forms and manifestations].

– 1 JOHN 1:7

November 21

I HAVE PUT MY CLOTHES ON YOU – righteousness, purity, destiny, dreams, holiness, steadfastness, courage, and peace. Trade these clothes for the tattered and torn items of your former life. I love you, child. Do not ever lose sight of that. I am a perfectly patient father. I will meet you where you are. It is impossible to change your spiritual clothes prior to coming to me because I am the one who provides the new ones.

My arms are open to you. I am not afraid of getting my hands dirty. Just take a step toward me and I will run to you! My love brings transformation.

I will rejoice greatly in the Lord, my soul will exult in my God; for He has clothed me with garments of salvation, He has covered me with a robe of righteousness, as a bridegroom puts on a turban, and as a bride adorns herself with her jewels.

– ISAIAH 61:10

November 22

I AM HERE. I AM ALWAYS HERE. You are becoming alive to that very reality. I love you and smile when I look at you. How I have longed to be a part of your every moment. But I can only be a part of the moments you invite me into. Thank you for inviting me to be a part of your life. Get ready, because you are going to know me in ways that you have not before. I am pouring my heart into yours in ways I could not before.

Pay attention. Are you awake? Let me wake you up in my glory. Dream dreams, see visions, and know that I am the God of the living. I am not the God of the dead. I am the God of the moment, the God of the now.

'And it shall be in the last days,' says God, that I will pour out My Spirit upon all mankind; and your sons and your daughters shall prophesy, and your young men shall see [divinely prompted] visions, and your old men shall dream [divinely prompted] dreams.

– ACTS 2:17

November 23

SHAPES CAN SHIFT AND CHANGE like clouds in the sky. Keep watching and seeing, for the end result is not always what it was in the beginning. Be patient and wait for things to take their final shape. While something may at first seem harsh, and may very well be, do not let that discourage you because it can become something soft and even snuggly.

I love the world. My tears are in it as well as my laughter. There are things that cause me so much joy, but other things cause me pain. The pain was never my intention. It is not what I want. My plan was to have only laughter and tears of joy. You can be a part of that plan. Plant your feet in my love and follow me as I show you how that love is lived out. Serve and elevate others above yourself.

I would have despaired had I not believed that I would see the goodness of the Lord in the land of the living. Wait for and confidently expect the Lord; be strong and let your heart take courage; yes, wait for and confidently expect the Lord.

– PSALM 27:13-14

November 24

WAIT, AND BE PATIENT FOR MY LEADING. Wait for my timing. I will not send you out until the time is right. Rest in knowing that I am ever mindful of you. Trust in the love I have for you. You know that I love and cherish you. Rest in that.

Wait for me to arrange the pieces that need to come together. I will exalt you at the right time. Keep seeking, praying, pursuing me, and loving others. Loving others will become natural as you continue to grow in the revelation of my love for you. You will only be able to love to the extent that you truly believe I love you. You have been changed and washed by my love, and you will continue to be. I love you so much. You are the sparkle in my eyes.

Dive deeper into the well of my love. I want you to experience everything that I am.

Bring all decision before me and seek my guidance and direction.

Humble yourselves [with an attitude of repentance and insignificance] in the presence of the Lord, and He will exalt you [He will lift you up, He will give you purpose].
– JAMES 4:10

❧ *November 25* ❧

FOLLOW ME RIGHT NOW IN THIS MOMENT. Do not be afraid. I am right here next to you; take my hand.

Consider a small trickle of water coming from the ground. It is seeping, but I see that it is about to burst forth like a geyser. Children are running to dance and play underneath the refreshing flow. Despair has turned to smiles and joy; hope has been realized. Dust and weariness has been washed away.

Breakthrough will come. Continue seeking me for direction. Do not move forward without my leading, for I will make a way where there seems to be no way; you must stay beside me in order to see it.

Arise [from spiritual depression to a new life], shine [be radiant with the glory and brilliance of the Lord]; for your light has come, and the glory and brilliance of the Lord has risen upon you.

– ISAIAH 60:1

❦ *November 26* ❧

GAZE UPON MY SMILE. I am love, not anger. I have flooded you with my love.

I will open the eyes of your heart in new ways. I want to bring you in even closer to my side. Listen for my laughter; listen for my joy. There are times when I laugh and you do not hear it. There have been times that I wanted to play, but you did not recognize it. I can be light and carefree. Those are important parts of my heart. I like to have fun. I am really cool to hang out with.

I love you. You are so precious to me. I have taken your hand and lifted you up. Be careful not to judge others. I have ascribed unsurpassable worth and value to everyone you see. When you look at the people around you, you are seeing a portion of me. I have made everyone in my image and likeness. I am the treasure inside of them that needs to be found. How you treat them is how you are treating me. How do you treat those around you?

The King will answer and say to them, 'I assure you and most solemnly say to you, to the extent that you did it for one of these brothers of Mine, even the least of them, you did it for Me.'
– MATTHEW 25:40

❧ *November 27* ❧

THOSE WHO HAVE THEIR IDENTITY, worth, and value wholly in me are free from the fangs of jealously and envy. Truth brings freedom and abundant LIFE. Expose the lies and find the truth I have planted in your heart. It is no longer you who lives, but me who lives in you. We live together.

Consider mountain peaks covered in ice and snow. There are many mountain peaks around you. They are people who have allowed their hearts to grow as cold as ice. They are hard and unmoving. But my love is the answer. It is the ray of hope straight from the only source hot enough to melt the coldest heart. I want you to carry this love for me. Take it to those desperate for warmth. Are you willing to do this?

Do nothing from selfishness or empty conceit [through factional motives, or strife], but with [an attitude of] humility [being neither arrogant nor self-righteous], regard others as more important than yourselves. Do not merely look out for your own personal interests, but also for the interests of others.

– PHILIPPIANS 2:3-4

November 28

LET ME FILL YOU WITH MY LIFE. I often appear dressed in the garments of people's perceptions. But I want you to see me clothed in the garments of love. Let love color your perception of me and the way in which you view the world. Let me appear in love and I will lead you into the truth of what love looks like lived out.

I am a deep well. Even deeper than you know or can understand at this time. The deeper you go, the more wonderful the experience. The water inside is cool, crisp, and invigorating. Ask me and I will take you there; I will broaden your understanding of who I am.

Beyond all these things put on and wrap yourselves in [unselfish] love, which is the perfect bond of unity [for everything is bound together in agreement when each one seeks the best for others].

– COLOSSIANS 3:14

❧ *November 29* ☙

PICTURE A SPARKLER, which looks like a dull stick without purpose before it is lit. It takes just a tiny flame to cause it to burst into marvelous colors and bright light. You have thought of yourself as dull and without purpose. Though I have never seen you this way, it has become your reality because of what you have chosen to believe at different times in your life.

A single flicker of my fire will ignite you in a way that will leave you, and those around you, amazed. You have the potential and components to stand out and shine brightly. Will you let my flame set fire to your being?

For God, who said, "Let light shine out of darkness," is the One who has shone in our hearts to give us the Light of the knowledge of the glory and majesty of God [clearly revealed] in the face of Christ.

– 2 CORINTHIANS 4:6

November 30

I WILL MAKE MY GLORY FALL on your head like rain. It will not stop at your head, but will caress your entire being. Every cell will come alive with me. Do you not know that I am with you? I am working to bring about all that you have requested, and even more of what you did not think to ask for.

I have in my hands two loaves of fresh bread. One is for right now, and one is for the days ahead. It is the bread of LIFE as it comes from me. I am your bread of LIFE today, and I will be your bread of LIFE tomorrow. Feed on me and you will always have everything you need.

Lift up your heads, O gates, and be lifted up, ancient doors, that the King of glory may come in. Who is the King of glory? The Lord strong and mighty, the Lord mighty in battle.

– PSALM 24:7-8

This page intentionally left blank

December

And [I pray] that the eyes of your heart
[the very center and core of your being]
may be enlightened [flooded with light
by the Holy Spirit], so that you will
know and cherish the hope [the divine
guarantee, the confident expectation]
to which He has called you, the riches
of His glorious inheritance in the saints
(God's people).

– EPHESIANS 1:18

December 1

I AM MOVING IN YOUR MIDST. There are times that you walk around with closed eyes and you cannot see what I am doing. Open up your eyes and you will see the marvelous things I have done for you. Take a moment to notice all of the blessings I have placed around you. Let it be your desire to be grateful, for thankfulness is a weapon against discouragement. Your adversary wants you to focus on what you do not have, but if you allow me to make your vision clear, you will find that you are in the center of abundance.

I am the well spring of LIFE bursting from the innermost parts of who you are. I am growing in you and soon your exterior will be bursting with LIFE as the interior will be completely transformed into my image. I have taken your ashes and given you beauty. Heaviness shall no longer weigh on your shoulders. You twinkle like the stars in the night sky.

And [I pray] that the eyes of your heart [the very center and core of your being] may be enlightened [flooded with light by the Holy Spirit], so that you will know and cherish the hope [the divine guarantee, the confident expectation] to which He has called you, the riches of His glorious inheritance in the saints (God's people).

– EPHESIANS 1:18

❦ *December 2* ❧

I AM LIKE A CINNAMON ROLL – sweet all the way through. The great thing is that you can eat as much of me as you want without having to worry about getting a stomach ache.

My light is shining on you. Walk in that knowledge and do not allow the enemy to gather the clouds above your head. Fix your eyes on me and you will hear the truth that will keep the sun shining down on you.

I am the light of the world, but I become distorted and misunderstood when viewed through the lenses of many different sunglasses. Who I want to be in your life, and in the lives of others, ends up being a shaded misperception of who I am. I want you to take off the sunglasses and help others do the same. The truth that I am love will remove the lens from cloudy eyes. There is no pain or suffering in me. There is healing, restoration, redemption, and acceptance. Run into my open arms!

Therefore let us [with privilege] approach the throne of grace [that is, the throne of God's gracious favor] with confidence and without fear, so that we may receive mercy [for our failures] and find [His amazing] grace to help in time of need [an appropriate blessing, coming just at the right moment].

– HEBREWS 4:16

BE IN THE WORLD, but do not become part of the world. Be transformed into my image by the renewing of your mind, and do not become conformed to the patterns of this world. I have called you to be set apart for me so that I can accomplish every good work I want to pour through you.

Do not resist my efforts to build relationship between you and the people around you, regardless of their beliefs. Do not become like oil is to water. Instead, be like the yeast that is added to dough that makes everything rise. Dough by itself becomes nothing. It needs to be changed in order to become something that is delicious and inviting. I want you to be that added ingredient so that I can bring those around you to LIFE.

Love others just as I have loved you, even those you consider the most difficult to love.

They are not of the world, just as I am not of the world. Sanctify them in the truth [set them apart for Your purposes, make them holy]; Your word is truth.

– JOHN 17:16-17

December 4

I AM WAITING HERE FOR YOU. Why do you reach out and look up when I am right in front of you? I am not positioned above you like a statue. I am with you. I came to earth to be with you. I get off of my throne to be with those I love.

Listen to my voice. Hear my sweet whispers into your ear. I will continually profess my love for you. You are my sweet bride and I love you so much. You are so precious to me. My arms are ever waiting for you. I will never draw them back. All you need to do is lift up your eyes and you will find me.

For I have come down from heaven, not to do My own will, but to do the will of Him who sent Me. This is the will of Him who sent Me, that of all that He has given Me I lose nothing, but that I [give new life and] raise it up at the last day.

– JOHN 6:38-39

December 5

YOU ARE AN AMAZING PERSON. I have given you so many unique gifts and abilities. But there are also areas to work on – things that can become a snare. I want you to rise above those potential snares as you seek my kingdom first. If you do, everything else will be added to you.

Let me drain away all of the mucky water that has threatened to rise above your head. I will restore LIFE to the things you thought were beyond saving. There is nothing beyond saving with me. In me, all things are possible. Do not lose hope. Do not lower your eyes because when you do, you lose sight of me. Draw strength from me, for I am so close to you, closer than you think. I will restore unto you the joy of your salvation.

Restore to me the joy of Your salvation and sustain me with a willing spirit.

– PSALM 52:12

❧ *December 6* ❧

DRINK FROM THE WATER I AM POURING against your lips. Feel it refresh and anoint you for the work I have called you to do. The work I have for you is to believe. I am calling you into LIFE. Do not stand at the door and refuse to cross the threshold. Put one foot in front of the other and come to me with open arms. Come to me without a timid heart. Come to me in the midst of fear. Come to me with your reservations. Just come.

I have cleared a spot for you right here next to me. There is no need to fear. You will discover that quickly as you begin to understand the depths of my consuming love for you. Consuming – that is what I want to be for you. I want to consume everything in your life because I have abundant LIFE waiting to replace it all. Will you trade the temporary things for the things that are eternal?

Then they asked Him, "What are we to do, so that we may habitually be doing the works of God?" Jesus answered, "This is the work of God: that you believe [adhere to, trust in, rely on, and have faith] in the One whom He has sent."

– JOHN 6:28-29

December 7

THERE IS NO SEPARATION BETWEEN US. You are filled with my spirit and I have equipped you to do great things. I will reveal to you what those things are in due time. Watch for the doors I open. Approach them from a place of rest and stay connected to my voice. I am in you and I am holding you together. All things are held together by my hand.

Do not pursue the things that stretch out to the right or to the left. I will align the things I have for you in front of you so that you can walk straight and possess them. You do not have to veer off of the path to find the things I have prepared for you. Do not chance those trails. They will lead you into deep wilderness.

For I am convinced [and continue to be convinced—beyond any doubt] that neither death, nor life, nor angels, nor principalities, nor things present and threatening, nor things to come, nor powers, nor height, nor depth, nor any other created thing, will be able to separate us from the [unlimited] love of God, which is in Christ Jesus our Lord.

– ROMANS 8:38-39

December 8

I AM INVITING YOU IN TO REST AND BE WITH ME.
If you stand at the door, your portion will be small and there will
be no intimacy. Know me from within and not from afar. I want
you to grasp my nature and character. See and perceive; hear and
understand.

I am breaking down your hard outer shell and getting into the
depths of who you really are. There have been times that you have
been afraid to show me who you are because you thought I would
not accept it. I have already accepted you – all of you. The things
that need to be cleaned up do not keep me from you. They do
not keep my arms from holding you tight. View yourself through
my eyes of love and you will find your feet carrying you into my
presence. There is no greater place for you!

*So he got up and came to his father. But while he was still a long
way off, his father saw him and was moved with compassion for
him, and ran and embraced him and kissed him.*

– LUKE 15:20

December 9

THOUGH THE RULER OF THE WORLD may come against you, there is no weapon formed against you that shall prosper. I will turn back every word spoken against you. The agents of oppression that lie in wait for you shall be overthrown. Your battle is not against flesh and blood but against the spiritual forces of darkness. They will be exposed by my light and they shall not bring you to ruin.

Do not fight the battles according to the rules of the natural world around you. The weapon you need to be successful is not made to destroy flesh and blood. The sword you hold is radiating with my love. It is my word and my power. It will consume all attacks, schemes, and devices the enemy has. It is mighty for the destruction of lies in you and around you. Let it shine bright and be a beacon for yourself and others.

"No weapon that is formed against you will succeed; and every tongue that rises against you in judgment you will condemn. This [peace, righteousness, security, and triumph over opposition] is the heritage of the servants of the Lord, and this is their vindication from Me," says the Lord.

– ISAIAH 54:17

December 10

I FLOW LIKE A RIVER DOWN STREETS that ring with praise. Come now and let us worship together. Let me adore you as you stand in my presence. Get lost in my arms as we dance to music I created just for you. You are a sweet fragrance that I love to breathe deeply. You are mine and I am yours. Take my hand and let me lead you into the joy and goodness I have prepared for you. The lilies of the field are nothing in beauty compared to you.

I have clothed you in beautiful robes of righteousness and purity. Return to the joy of your youth. I can restore all that has been lost. There are times that it seems like joy is hiding from you, that you cannot seem to find your way to the peace I speak so much about. Keep your eyes on me and listen to my voice. I am wiping away the gritty shame that has piled on your heart. I am removing the extra baggage that has weighed you down. Let me take it. I really will if you let me.

O come, let us worship and bow down, let us kneel before the Lord our Maker [in reverent praise and prayer].
— PSALM 95:6

December 11

SOME MOUNTAINS LOOK STURDY on the outside but crumble at the slightest shake. Others look meek and small but can stand against the greatest of quakes. You are strong because I am strong in you. You will stand against the most powerful tremors because I am alive and active in you.

But if you ever begin to believe that you are standing under your own power, you will start to crumble. The moment you start believing that your own intelligence can untangle the issues in your life, the net will tighten. You need me to fortify you from the inside out and that is what I am doing. I have given you wisdom that will always be available to you. Do not be afraid. I am waking you up to my voice so that I can guide you through the decisions that need to be made.

My flesh and my heart may fail, but God is the rock and strength of my heart and my portion forever.

– PSALM 73:26

December 12

I LOVE YOU. I AM YOURS, and you are mine. I have a bucket of love that is constantly pouring out on you. You are always being completely saturated with it even when you do not feel it. You cannot escape it. I will pursue you across the greatest desert. There is nothing that will ever keep me from trying to draw you into my arms. I will never turn my back and give up on you. You have experienced the failure of those around you, but I will never let you down. I am the answer for everything your heart longs for. I created you for my arms. You fit perfectly in me.

Just keep putting one foot in front of the other and follow my voice. I am all around you. Do not be afraid, for I am setting your heart on fire in order to blaze the trail I have for you. But you will never have to walk the path alone. I am always here.

Let us approach [God] with a true and sincere heart in unqualified assurance of faith, having had our hearts sprinkled clean from an evil conscience and our bodies washed with pure water.

– HEBREWS 10:22

❦ December 13 ❦

NO MATTER WHAT HAPPENS, do not allow the hope I have placed inside of you to be stolen. Do not lose heart even when it seems so hard to connect with me. We connect in many ways that you do not see. I do not wait for you to think of me before I come by your side. I am not standing in another room waiting for you to talk to me before I move. I am always here no matter what, and I am always working for you. Keep the flame of your hope fed by the knowledge of how much I love you.

The world needs to see genuine, sincere love. There is not a heart out there that will not be impacted by my love. It is not too late for anyone. Even in the worst pain imaginable, the slightest glimmer of sincere love has the power to break through. Be a reflection of that love. Let your life be a testimony of what I have to offer.

I am giving you a new commandment, that you love one another. Just as I have loved you, so you too are to love one another. By this everyone will know that you are My disciples, if you have love and unselfish concern for one another."

– JOHN 13:34-35

December 14

THE COOL WATERS I BRING DO NOT TASTE BITTER. They do not taste of strife and they do not bring anxiety. The waters I bring are peaceful and will refresh you.

Step out of the troubled waters that have gathered around you. Take my hand and I will support your feet so that you can not only escape from the storms that have come, but also walk right on top of the raging sea. See, even in the midst of hard times I can bring a calm that will allow you to recognize that there is a way out. Do not focus on the waves that seek to capsize you. Instead, listen to my voice as I reassure you that it is going to be okay. Keep your eyes on me and not on the circumstances fighting to rob you of peace. You cannot do it on your own, but with me you can be more than a conqueror. Your enemy wants you to focus on the hopelessness the dark clouds bring. I want you to focus on the LIFE my smile brings.

"For I the Lord your God keep hold of your right hand; [I am the Lord], who says to you, 'Do not fear, I will help you.'

– ISAIAH 41:13

December 15

THERE ARE MANY WHO KNOW what my voice of comfort sounds like. There are many who know what my voice of peace, wisdom and guidance sounds like. Many people know and recognize my voice but few know and recognize my laughter. Do you know what my laughter sounds like?

I am the God who laughs. There is exceeding joy in my heart and I want you to see it; I want you to experience it. The amount of celebration that goes on in my kingdom would shock you. There is a time to grieve and there is a time to laugh. But many do not seem to recognize the times to laugh with me. Do you recognize those times?

I will lift up your head with just one touch from my hand. You are the sparkle in my eye and I am the laughter in your heart. I am the fullness within you. I am the source of your LIFE.

Then our mouth was filled with laughter and our tongue with joyful shouting; then they said among the nations, "The Lord has done great things for them."

– PSALM 126:2

❧ *December 16* ❧

I LOVE YOU. I AM YOUR STRONG TOWER. Hold fast to me and you shall not come to ruin. The winds can blow and the ground can shake, but I will not let you crumble to the ground. But in the times that you let your hand slip from mine, do not be afraid. Do not consider it all lost. I will restore you – put you back together again. I am the rain drops on your face sending torrents of refreshment through you. I am enough for you.

Be steadfast – pure in heart and motive. I am coming; I am coming for my beautiful bride. You are the bride. Do not take the beautiful gown I have draped over your shoulders out to play in the mud. Never run from correction, but embrace it. It leads to LIFE.

Blessed [anticipating God's presence, spiritually mature] are the pure in heart [those with integrity, moral courage, and godly character], for they will see God.

– MATTHEW 5:8

December 17

YOU ARE FIRMLY PLANTED IN MY GARDEN OF LIFE. I tend you carefully, pulling out the weeds that creep in. I love your beautiful and unique expressions. I am constantly checking your root system and making sure the soil is rich and full of LIFE. I am not the gardener out of a sense of obligatory duty, but out of pleasure and joy. I love walking through the unique plants. Each one tantalizes my senses.

But some of your tendrils have wrapped very tightly around a couple of weeds because you think that you need them, that they add LIFE to you, that they can nourish you. In cases like this, the entanglement is so intricately woven that I cannot simply pry you apart. You must release the weed before I can remove it. The weed might make you feel good for a short time, but only I can bring you the LIFE you were created for. Wrap every tendril around me. What will you choose?

The righteous will flourish like the date palm [long-lived, upright and useful]; they will grow like a cedar in Lebanon [majestic and stable]. Planted in the house of the Lord, they will flourish in the courts of our God.

– PSALM 92:12-13

December 18

I AM STANDING WITH YOU IN A COURTROOM.
Your adversary has dragged you here, but the tables are about to be reversed. There are no stains that remain on you and I have taken the voice of your accuser. How dare your adversary bring you in front me to be accused. It shall not be. I am your defender, your attorney; I will set you free in the revelation that you are, in fact, free.

Your adversary has handed you dirty rags to wear and you have put them on because you thought you were not worth anything more. But I have removed those tattered garments and supplied you with white robes of righteousness and purity. Yes, I said purity. I have cleansed you of everything that would cause spot or wrinkle. If you can accept this, you can put on the clothes I have given you and take your rightful place by my side. Yes, I really do love you that much. Will you join me?

Purify me with hyssop, and I will be clean; wash me, and I will be whiter than snow.

– PSALM 51:7

December 19

I AM SO FULL OF JOY FOR YOU. You are my delight. Do you really get that? I will say it again so you can be sure to hear it. I delight in you; you make my heart dance. You are so beautiful to me. The work of your hands crafts a song of praise that glorifies my name.

LIFE comes from whatever I touch. Extend your heart to me and I will fill it with abundant LIFE. Trade your sorrows for my joy and your heaviness for my garment of praise. I will make your steps light. I am the one who calls to you, encouraging you to take one more step. I am the strength you need to move forward. I am shining like the sun even in the darkest night. There is no circumstance that is beyond hope. Get to know the fullness of who I am so that I can be a present help in time of need. Will you let me help you? I will open the doors that lead to your dreams.

You have turned my mourning into dancing for me; You have taken off my sackcloth and clothed me with joy.

– PSALM 30:11

December 20

I HAVE BIRTHED DREAMS, VISIONS, and goals in your heart. Pursue them with eagerness, but walk alongside me. You are not the only one who wants the desires of your heart to be fulfilled. You are not the only one who wants you to step into your dreams, or who wants the deepest longings of your heart to become a reality in your life. I want all of those things for you, and I want them even more than you do.

Come alive with me! Put down everything that seeks to hold you in place. You do not need many of the things you think you need. Get ready to make a list and I will light up your mind with the things you should leave behind. They will be things you count on to give you temporary satisfaction and relief. They are the things getting in the way of the true LIFE I have for you. Take courage, and eliminate the things keeping you from the deeper path I have for you.

May He grant you your heart's desire and fulfill all your plans. We will sing joyously over your victory, and in the name of our God we will set up our banners. May the Lord fulfill all your petitions.

– PSALM 20:4-5

December 21

I AM RAISING YOU UP AS A TRUMPET OF MY WORD. The sound of your voice shall carry mine into the darkness that gathers. My voice is a hammer against hard stone. It chips and finally breaks the stone away to reveal the gold inside.

Let me make your heart soft like mine. It can grow hard, which is why you need to let my love lead you and let it continually pour over you. The distractions of the world seek to pull you away from my voice, but I will gather you in my arms like a shepherd gathers his sheep. Do not stray from the path I have marked out for you because wolves travel back and forth on either side waiting to devour those who wander off on their own.

I am your fortress and strong tower. I will keep you safe and I will restore your soul. Your spirit cannot help but be lifted in me. But you must make the choice to enter into my presence. I want to be all you need. Will you let me?

Moreover, I will give you a new heart and put a new spirit within you, and I will remove the heart of stone from your flesh and give you a heart of flesh.

– EZEKIEL 36:26

December 22

BREATHE WITH ME. Rest on my stomach and listen to my heart beat. Feel my chest rise and fall. There is nothing else that you should be doing right now. All of the other stuff can wait. Slow down and just be with me.

Every promise is fulfilled in me. Share in my LIFE and receive everything I have for you. Do not let discouragement tear you down. Discouragement is like a swarm of locusts intent on destroying what you have achieved. But be encouraged by my love for you. I am holding you tight in my arms. You are already a success.

Listen closely and you will be able to hear the song I am singing over you. I will teach you the words. It is a song of celebration!

For as many as are the promises of God, in Christ they are [all answered] "Yes." So through Him we say our "Amen" to the glory of God.

– 1 CORINTHIANS 1:20

December 23

I AM THE ONLY WELL OF LIFE, and I never run dry. The water inside is liquid joy. Those who drink of me find what they have been missing. They find the joy that was a mystery to them. It begins to rise in them like an elevator until it bursts forth in waves of laughter. The only true laughter is that which comes from the depths of my heart. All other laughter rings hollow and empty.

This joy is part of the treasure I have for you. And it is only a portion of all I have for you. There is so much more. I have deposited an abundance of LIFE into the plans I have for you. Keep your heart open to me. That LIFE will always be available to you. I will help you find it but I will not pull you. Wherever you plant your feet is where you will stay. Will you plant your feet in me?

Jesus answered her, "Everyone who drinks this water will be thirsty again. But whoever drinks the water that I give him will never be thirsty again. But the water that I give him will become in him a spring of water [satisfying his thirst for God] welling up [continually flowing, bubbling within him] to eternal life."

– JOHN 4:13-14

December 24

I AM THE LORD YOUR GOD, AND I LOVE YOU. You are precious to me. Do not ever grow weary of hearing that from me. Do not take those words for granted. Take it to heart; I am LIFE.

I enjoy you and I love being with you. You make my eyes sparkle. Your struggles are not unknown to me, but I want you to know that my grace is sufficient for you. I have given you power and authority out of that grace to know the truth. You shall stomp on the heads of snakes and scorpions with that truth. It is not by might or power, but by my spirit of truth that you will experience victory. I am the truth, the way, and the LIFE.

The sum of Your word is truth [the full meaning of all Your precepts], and every one of Your righteous ordinances endures forever.

– PSALM 119:160

THERE HAVE BEEN TIMES that you have wondered if I am really here for you. The ground has seemed to crack under your feet and you felt the air whip by as if you were in a freefall. But what you can see with your eyes, and how you feel, is not always an accurate picture of reality.

I want you to know that I am your staff. I am your rock, your support, and your strong tower. Gravel and slippery rocks are strewn across the path ahead, but if you wait for me, I will clear them away and the path will be smooth. Have patience and listen to my voice of wisdom. Pay attention to the promptings of my spirit as I lead you. It is not by might or by power, but by my spirit.

Then he said to me, "This [continuous supply of oil] is the word of the Lord to Zerubbabel [prince of Judah], saying, 'Not by might, nor by power, but by My Spirit [of whom the oil is a symbol],' says the Lord of hosts.

– ZECHARIAH 4:6

December 26

THERE IS A CROWN THAT RESTS ON MY HEAD, but it is not just mine. I have chosen to share it with you because it brings me pleasure to see you glorified and lifted up. I love you. You make me laugh and your heart is refreshing. Remember the words I have spoken to you and over you. Watch them come to pass and know that I keep my promises. My love is real, alive, and active in you.

You are pure; I want you to remain in my purity. Step where I step and go where I go. Listen to and value the people I have placed around you. Love them as I love them. Let the development of relationship be one of your highest goals. When you get tired, I will hold you and blow LIFE into your weary bones. I will be everything you need for the days ahead. Stay close to my side. I am so excited to reveal all I have for you.

In the future there is reserved for me the [victor's] crown of righteousness [for being right with God and doing right], which the Lord, the righteous Judge, will award to me on that [great] day—and not to me only, but also to all those who have loved and longed for and welcomed His appearing.

– 2 TIMOTHY 4:8

December 27

IT IS OKAY, MY CHILD. I am right here with you, and I love you immensely. My arms are around you right now. Look today for the joy I provide and you shall find it everywhere you go. Even in the midst of heartache you can see my love and joy shining through the clouds. Let my joy be your strength today.

I am not asking you to forget the pain and trials. I know they are very real. I am asking you to realize who I am in the midst of everything else. I have overcome. Dive into my heart and experience the well spring of LIFE.

And [that you may come] to know [practically, through personal experience] the love of Christ which far surpasses [mere] knowledge [without experience], that you may be filled up [throughout your being] to all the fullness of God [so that you may have the richest experience of God's presence in your lives, completely filled and flooded with God Himself].
                                                    – EPHESIANS 3:19

December 28

I AM CONSTANTLY SHINING ON YOU; my face lights up when I think about you. You do not know how much I love you. I want you to understand that my love is not swayed by the things you do or do not do. I cannot help but smile at you.

When you get dirty, I want to make you clean, and I do every time you come to me. But if you believe you are still dirty after a spiritual shower, then that will be your reality. Many come to me repeatedly asking me to cleanse them from the same sin. They scrub themselves raw in an attempt to feel clean. Child, open your eyes, look in the mirror, and see through my eyes. You have already been made clean. Walk in the robes of righteousness that I have clothed you with. Let this be your reality!

"I, only I, am He who wipes out your transgressions for My own sake, and I will not remember your sins.

– ISAIAH 43:25

December 29

BE AWARE OF MY VOICE, because I am a chatterbox. I am always speaking and doing something. I never watch things play out from the sidelines. I am doing whatever I can to get in the game. But I see that sometimes clouds gather over your head. Lighting and thunder flash and crash, and your ears are deafened to my voice. But you do not have to settle for that. Take the power and authority I have given you and command the storm to be silent. Then focus on my voice and you will hear the words I have for you.

Listen to what I am telling you so that I can make a difference. Remember that you are always being washed and tossed in the ocean of my love. My waters are never stagnant; they will lead you to LIFE.

Encourage the exhausted, and make staggering knees firm. Say to those with an anxious and panic-stricken heart, "Be strong, fear not! Indeed, your God will come with vengeance [for the ungodly]; the retribution of God will come, but He will save you." Then the eyes of the blind will be opened and the ears of the deaf will be unstopped.

– ISAIAH 35:3-5

❧[*December 30*]☙

IT IS OKAY. I am right here with you; I love you. My arms are around you right now. Look for the peace and joy I provide that transcends all circumstances, and you shall find it. You can see my love surrounding you even in the midst of heartache. My joy is your strength. It does not mean forgetting – it means realizing who I am in the midst of everything else. I have overcome; I have overcome; I have overcome. Dive into my heart and experience the well spring of LIFE that is within.

It is in the difficult times that you might want to grasp onto something in the natural to distract you enough to make you feel good. But that can only be temporary relief that will only leave you feeling hungry, and may even open your heart to shame. Grasp onto me instead, and let me lead you. I will carry you through the hard times. Do not reach for worldly things around you to be your source of hope and strength. You do not need those things. You need my heart, and it is open for you.

And the peace of God [that peace which reassures the heart, that peace] which transcends all understanding, [that peace which] stands guard over your hearts and your minds in Christ Jesus [is yours].

– PHILIPPIANS 4:7

December 31

I AM RENEWING YOU EVERY DAY. I am revealing more of myself to you all of the time. That is how you will grow with me and know me in greater ways. The days are new every morning and the revelation I will give you will be fresh and new.

Continue to follow me every day this coming year. You will need my strength. Take my courage and my love and show it to the world. I have fashioned you after what I have determined *normal* should be. Do not allow anyone or anything to fashion you in a different way.

Many will come alive this coming year. Some you will see, but many you will not. But I am always working and moving in the lives of my children. Take your steps slowly as one who walks with much wisdom and discernment. If you walk slowly, you will see the path laid out before you. Let's venture the road together.

It is because of the Lord's loving kindnesses that we are not consumed, because His [tender] compassions never fail. They are new every morning; great and beyond measure is Your faithfulness.

– LAMENTATIONS 22-23

More from Jesse Birkey

Marriage What's the Point? One Couple Finds Meaning in a Crazy Mess
Jesse and Kara share the testimony of their marriage with bold transparency. Draw encouragement and hope from their story as God brought them from the depths of despair into the joy of restoration.

....

Life Resurrected, Extraordinary Miracles through Ordinary People
The dead come to life as ordinary people discover we all have the ability to live the extraordinary life of Jesus.

....

Finding Home. Book One in The Lost and Found Series
John had been a pillar in his local church, but the loss of his family in a terrible accident destroyed all he'd known to be true. After cutting ties with everyone and moving across the country, he settled into a life of alcohol, women, and bar fights. Can a surprising move and chance at love finally bring light to the darkness?

....

Available at www.jessebirkey.com and www.amazon.com

Jesse Birkey
PO Box 816
Riverview, FL 33568

Join the Conversation
Visit and interact with Jesse and Kara at:
www.jessebirkey.com

Connect with Jesse and Kara
jbirkey@jessebirky.com
https://www.facebook.com/jbirk
https://www.twitter.com/jessebirkey

Made in the USA
Las Vegas, NV
13 March 2022